Working Together

Working Together

Practicing the Science of Diversity, Equity, and Inclusion

Mikki Hebl & Eden King

OXFORD
UNIVERSITY PRESS

Oxford University Press is a department of the University of Oxford. It furthers the University's objective of excellence in research, scholarship, and education by publishing worldwide. Oxford is a registered trade mark of Oxford University Press in the UK and certain other countries.

Published in the United States of America by Oxford University Press
198 Madison Avenue, New York, NY 10016, United States of America.

© Oxford University Press 2024

All rights reserved. No part of this publication may be reproduced, stored in a retrieval system, or transmitted, in any form or by any means, without the prior permission in writing of Oxford University Press, or as expressly permitted by law, by license, or under terms agreed with the appropriate reproduction rights organization. Inquiries concerning reproduction outside the scope of the above should be sent to the Rights Department, Oxford University Press, at the address above.

You must not circulate this work in any other form
and you must impose this same condition on any acquirer.

Library of Congress Cataloging-in-Publication Data
Names: Hebl, Mikki, editor. | King, Eden, editor.
Title: Working together : Practicing the Science of Diversity, Equity, and Inclusion / Mikki Hebl & Eden King.
Description: New York, NY : Oxford University Press, [2024] |
Includes bibliographical references and index. |
Identifiers: LCCN 2023040478 (print) | LCCN 2023040479 (ebook) |
ISBN 9780197744383 (hardback) | ISBN 9780197744406 (epub) |
ISBN 9780197744413
Subjects: LCSH: Diversity in the workplace. | Interpersonal relations. |
Personnel management. | Discrimination in employment—Prevention.
Classification: LCC HF5549.5.M5 W673 2024 (print) |
LCC HF5549.5.M5 (ebook) | DDC 658.3008—dc23/eng/20231026
LC record available at https://lccn.loc.gov/2023040478
LC ebook record available at https://lccn.loc.gov/2023040479

DOI: 10.1093/oso/9780197744383.001.0001

Printed by Sheridan Books, Inc., United States of America

Contents

List of Figures and Tables   vii
Foreword   ix
   Melonie Parker
Acknowledgments   xi
About the Authors   xiii

Introduction   1

SECTION 1. THE WHAT AND WHY OF WORKING TOGETHER

1. What Is Diversity?   11
2. The Realistic Imperative of Diversity   18
3. The Financial Imperative of Diversity   29
4. The Moral Imperative of Diversity   39
5. Are There Downsides to Diversity?   44

SECTION 2. BIASES THAT HOLD US BACK FROM WORKING TOGETHER

6. Psychological Explanations for Bias   55
7. Individual-Level Discrimination   70
8. Organization-Level Discrimination   86

SECTION 3. STRATEGIES TO HELP US WORK TOGETHER

9. What Can Individual Targets of Discrimination Do?   99
10. What Can Allies Do?   112
11. What Can Organizations Do?   128

SECTION 4. MUST DO'S FOR LEADING A DIVERSE WORKFORCE TOGETHER

12. The Attraction–Selection–Attrition Model Applied to Working Together — 145
13. Increasing Diversity, Equity, and Inclusion in Employee Attraction — 150
14. Enhancing Diversity, Equity, and Inclusion in Employee Selection — 161
15. Reducing Employee Attrition — 175
16. Final Reflections on Working Together — 197

Index — 203

Figures and Tables

Figures

6.1	Checker-shadow illusion	57
6.2	Checker-shadow illusion, cropped	57
6.3	Café wall optical illusion	59
6.4	Vehicle stereotypes	62
6.5	CEO stereotypes	62
6.6	Perceptions of warmth and competence	66
7.1	Am I mansplaining?	71
8.1	Modern Van Heusen clothing models	87
8.2	1950s Van Heusen racist advertisement	88
9.1	Participant in Madera and Hebl's (2019) study	104
9.2	Stigma acknowledgment across time of an interview	105
10.1	Configuration of participants in Asch's (1956) study	117
10.2	Example of lines from Asch's (1956) study	117
10.3	ALLIES acronym	125
11.1	Example of SWOT analysis worksheet	139
13.1	Websites depicting Black versus White employees	153
14.1	Cumulative lifetime earnings for men versus women	168
15.1	Focus areas of ERGs in surveyed companies	182
15.2	Examples of diversity-welcoming imagery	185
15.3	Examples of diversity-forward accolades	186
15.4	Examples of LGBTQ+ positive campaigns	187

Tables

6.1	Labels for Stern Male and Female Leaders	63
15.1	Diversity Training Myths	190
15.2	Inequitable Example of Diversity Spread Within an Organization	195
15.3	Equitable Example of Diversity Spread Within an Organization	195

Foreword

Recently, I had the opportunity to visit George Floyd Square in Minneapolis, Minnesota, and stand on the ground where he was murdered. Reflecting on this experience left me with two thoughts. First, the ordinary setting for this extraordinary event was a reminder of how deeply systemic racism permeates every aspect of life and how we will need determination and tenacity to unroot it. Second, the continued outpouring of handmade signs and community gardens, 3 years later, was a reminder of the endurance required to ensure this is not a moment, but a movement.

Diversity, equity, and inclusion have never been about a moment in time but a momentum that catalyzes a collective set of actions focused on ensuring that those who have historically been denied full participation in the workforce have the same opportunities as their peers. What are we solving for, one might ask? In the Declaration of Independence, there is an iconic phrase written by Thomas Jefferson that states, "All men are created equal." This nation was founded on principles that included the idea that all people are created equal and have fundamental rights, promising liberty and equality for all. The Fourteenth Amendment to the United States Constitution declares that the states must provide all people equal treatment under the law. These statements reference the promise of equal outcomes; however, neither of these declarations makes reference to the lived experiences, social determinants, or comorbidities that contextualize the outcomes for marginalized communities and underrepresented individuals. We have to acknowledge our society's long history of ebbs and flows that have negatively impacted civil rights progress.

It's not lost on me that in 2024, we can predict the health outcomes, well-being, and success of individuals based on the zip code they are born into. Findings in the "Root Causes of Health" report by

Healthbox explored the idea that your zip code can carry more weight on your potential health outcomes than your genetic code. The social determinants that undergird this research are the same comorbidities that undergird communities that have historically been denied full participation in the workforce.

George Floyd's murder caught on video forced us to watch an unconscionable act of violence that compelled us to deepen our commitment to diversity, equity, and inclusion. This deepened commitment highlighted the role of leaders whose responsibility it is to steward progress toward closing gaps to parity in the workforce across hiring, promotions, retention, and lived experiences. Who takes on the leadership role for ensuring that we live up to the principles of diversity, equity, inclusion, accessibility, and belonging for all individuals, both inside and outside of the company? Who is the bellwether that helps ensure the appropriate focus, actions, and progress? This is the responsibility of leaders.

Working Together: Practicing the Science of Diversity, Equity, and Inclusion is designed to help all leaders understand diversity, equity, and inclusion on a personal and introspective level and at an organizational level. This book shines light on biases that impact every facet of life, including the workplace. This is a key inflection point in our nation's history, and leaders have the opportunity and responsibility to ensure that diversity, equity, and inclusion principles are embedded in business strategies, policies, approaches, and principles. Furthermore, leaders have the stewardship responsibility to model the actions and behaviors that we all need to embrace.

This work is not about ensuring that we all feel warm and fuzzy inside through our goals of achieving a common humanity. This work is about reaching the aspirations set forth by the founding fathers of our nation; advancing work culture and experience through closing gaps to parity; and most of all ensuring the dignity, respect, and esteem of all individuals.

Melonie Parker

Acknowledgments

Our cups overflow with gratitude. We are grateful to the researchers on whose shoulders we stand, the friends and colleagues who kindly provided feedback, the MBA students who generously shared their experiences, the PhD and undergraduate students who helped us do the research we report in this book, and our families for inspiring us to make the world better.

About the Authors

Mikki Hebl is Professor of Psychology and Management at Rice University who joined the faculty at Rice University in 1998 and was given the endowed title of the Radoslav Tsanoff Assistant Professorship in 2000. Her research specifically focuses on workplace discrimination and the barriers stigmatized individuals (e.g., women and ethnic minorities) face in social interactions, the hiring process, business settings, and the medical community. In addition, she addresses ways in which both individuals and organizations might remediate such discrimination. She has more than 200 publications that include journal articles, book chapters, and edited books. In addition to conducting research, she is committed to translating her research findings to educate others and ameliorate disparate social inequities. She has been the recipient of 20 major teaching awards and was appointed "National Professor of the Year" in 2016.

Eden King is Professor of Industrial–Organizational Psychology at Rice University. She is pursuing a program of research that aims to make work better for everyone. This research—which has yielded more than 100 scholarly products and has been featured in outlets such as *The New York Times*, *Good Morning America*, and *Harvard Business Review*—addresses three primary themes: (1) current manifestations of discrimination and barriers to work–life balance in organizations, (2) consequences of such challenges for its targets and their workplaces, and (3) individual and organizational strategies for reducing discrimination and increasing support for families. In addition to her scholarship, she has partnered with organizations to improve diversity climate, increase fairness in selection systems, and design and implement diversity training programs. She is currently co-editor of the *Journal of Business and Psychology* and has served as President of the Society for Industrial–Organizational Psychology.

Introduction

We were prompted to write this book based on three recurring sets of questions from our various audiences, who range from undergraduates to executive MBA students, from entry-level workers to seasoned professionals, and from the general public to the C-suites of organizations.

The first set of questions we commonly get are "But don't people who work hard get ahead?" and "Why can't we just deal with diversity by operating under the principle of meritocracy?" Importantly, most people who ask these questions are sincere and well-intentioned; after all, they have worked hard, they have played by the rules, and—for the most part—they, themselves, have gotten ahead. These people reason that they have worked hard to earn advantages for themselves and their offspring, and others should be able to do the same, just as they have done. As a result, many of these individuals perceive that their own hard work leads them to positive outcomes, and it is others' lack of this hard work that leads to more negative outcomes.

Psychologists describe this set of beliefs as the "just-world phenomenon" or the tendency to believe that people get what they deserve and deserve what they get. This *belief* is associated with lived experiences that often divide those who have found success from those who have not. In addition, people tend to downplay the power of luck or fortunate circumstances in their own and others' lives; instead, those who are lucky are seen as being intrinsically talented, intelligent, and hardworking, and those who are not so lucky and/or who have misfortunes that befall them tend to be blamed for their outcomes or presumed to have just not tried hard enough.

A meritocratic ideal is sensible at first glance. Jobs, promotions, and resources should seemingly go to the best qualified, not to those who have the best background, money, or status. And these opportunities certainly should not go to people just because they have a certain skin color. The problem is what tends to happen under systems of meritocracy: Those who come from favored backgrounds, money, and status tend to benefit the most, and those who come from unprivileged backgrounds have far too much trouble escaping them and are stuck within structures that reinforce the status quo. The fact that everyone can think of someone their family or their family's neighbor might know or can name a few famous people who are the makings of rags-to-riches stories (e.g., Andrew Carnegie, Howard Schultz, John Paul DeJoria, Oprah Winfrey, and Sheldon Adleson) only further feeds the meritocracy narrative. The illusion of meritocracy is powerful. Metaphorically, people who are born on third base believe that they hit a triple to get there. These same people often believe that those who didn't make it to first base just didn't try hard enough. It is a case in which the rich often get richer, and the poor often get poorer. Those living in poverty, for instance, often do not have access to the better schools, medical care, and basic resources, so it is more difficult for them to catapult themselves into a higher social and financial category. As Abraham Maslow might say, these individuals are trying to fulfill their most basic needs. Meanwhile, the rich have much greater access and have their basic needs met, so they can focus on themselves and advancing.

In short, the meritocracy idea is a myth. And this book sets out to explain how a number of variables other than the combination of IQ and effort determine where you will end up in the organizational hierarchy. We look forward to teaching you about stereotypes, biases both overt and subtle, and other sets of beliefs which keep us from understanding that beliefs in the meritocracy hold us back from helping solve the problems associated with creating genuine fairness. We particularly look forward to doing this at a time when these constructs are often misconstrued and they and DEI initiatives more generally are under assault.

The second question we get asked so commonly is a variation on "What guide do you recommend in helping our organization with diversity?" and "What can we do at our workplace?" After listening to our talks, our audience members want the primer on how best to understand, think about, and realize diversity in their own organizations. Ultimately, what lies behind this question is a desire to have a digestible but also objective, empirically based account of how to best be intentional and deliberate about diversity in their own organizations.

Indeed, at the end of a talk we gave at a large customer event for Emerson Automation Solutions, a White male contractor in the far back of the room raised his hand during the Q & A. After waiting patiently for the microphone to reach him, he cleared his throat and asked, "What book do you recommend to teach others in our organization about all this diversity stuff?" The audience grew silent as they waited for us to respond. Unlike answers to the others' questions that came readily and fervently, we had no great recommendation. We paused and then answered honestly, "None that we know of." Certainly, there are many books (and good ones) that touch on some aspects of demography, advantages and disadvantages of diversity, bias, remediation strategies, and diversity management, but there are none that capture the totality of content that we have been researching about discrimination and advocating about diversity in organizations. Combining 60+ years of experience, ours and others' research findings, and compiled knowledge, we finally have a good answer to the man in the back of the room. *This* book is it.

Finally, the third set of questions comes from many of the employees, students, or other individuals in our audiences who are from groups that have been historically marginalized, targeted, and underrepresented. They ask, "How can we help, too?" and "Why strategies should we use to reduce bias and/or to make changes in our organizations?" They are exhausted but hopeful. They are beaten but alive. They are broken but still reaching. And they are resilient and want to contribute. This book is written for leaders and future leaders across industries, occupations, and levels. We include summaries of robust data together with powerful anecdotes to address the what, the why, and the how of diversity, equity, and inclusion (DEI). We explain what DEI is and why it matters, and offer individual and organizational strategies for changing organizations in ways that are more equitable, encompassing, and profitable, Each chapter ends with questions and activities that prompt readers to engage more deeply and reflect on their own experiences and workplaces.

To that end, there are several points that we make when we begin a new executive MBA class on diversity or give a diversity-related talk within our own or at other organizations. We include them here too, because they are critical elements of making the rest of the material in this book stick. And sticking is exactly what we want the contents of this book to do.

Share to Make It Stick

If you are reading this book because you hope to make some lasting organizational change, we have early advice for you. After you are finished reading this book, give it to others. In particular, give it to your manager, your manager's manager, and/or the chief executive officer (CEO) of your company. Then, make them promise to read it. Why? It is not for our own personal increase in revenue. It is because getting buy-in on diversity from members of top management is absolutely key to making any sort of lasting and institutional diversity-related changes in your organization. Study after study has shown that leaders are essential to making and expediting real change; leaders have the biggest input into setting the tone for an organization's diversity climate and diversity-related policies that trickle down to attract and retain the most talented people out there, diverse and not.

Eric Yuan, founder, chairman, and CEO of Zoom is an excellent example of this.[1,2] He turned a small company, Saasbee, into the giant

---

[1] Memis, H. (2020, April 3). *Saasbee to Zoom: The inspiring story of Zoom and its founder Eric Yuan*. LinkedIn. https://www.linkedin.com/pulse/saasbee-zoom-inspiring-story-its-founder-eric-yuan-halim-memi%C5%9F/?articleId=6652239384596877312.

[2] Stone, B. (2020, March 28). *A biography of Eric Yan, founder and CEO of Zoom*. Medium. https://medium.com/@brett.stone/a-biography-of-eric-yuan-founder-and-ceo-of-zoom-deec5b42c723.

video web-conferencing platform (now valued at more than $10 billion) that so many of us use today. Although he is known for his willingness to work hard and focus on developing excellent products, he is also known for his commitment to DEI. This reveals itself in his quality product, which provides people the opportunity to maintain social support and connection throughout the world. Eric is focused on both structural and cultural aspects of diversity. Structurally, he has established an internal DEI team, hosted town hall meetings to learn more, launched employee resource groups, built DEI initiatives into Zoom's hiring process, initiated partnerships to improve hiring equity, initiated an annual Care for All DEI report,[3] instituted Zoom talks (like TED talks) that focus on teaching others about diversity, and created a Zoom Cares philanthropic program. Culturally, he has partnered with leading experts to create educational programming for Zoom employees about workplace issues, voting rights, mental health, and racial trauma in the workplace. He has also signed partnerships with historically Black colleges and universities. It is not surprising that Eric won the top spot on the 2021 Comparably's Best CEO for Diversity,[4] achieving a diversity rating of 90/100 by his employees and a rating of a 98/100 by his non-White employees. His company has also consistently made Glassdoor's "Best Places to Work." The trickle-down effects of having leadership who believes in and prioritizes diversity and related initiatives is clear.

Therefore, make sure this book finds its way to the leader of your team, division, branch, and organization. If top management is not invested in making some changes and does not subscribe to the kind of scientific evidence present in this book, any sort of significant change is likely to be hampered. It is difficult enough to make changes without the leaders being onboard, but without their support, you are working from the bottom up. And working from this perspective is always much more difficult. You lack consolidated

---

[3] Zoom. (2022, Spring). *Care for All: Through Diversity, Equity & Inclusion: Inaugural DEI Report.* https://explore.zoom.us/media/zoom-dei-inaugural-report-spring-2022_final.pdf.
[4] Comparably. (2022). *Zoom wins top Comparably 2021 award for best CEO of diversity.* https://www.comparably.com/news/zoom-wins-top-comparably-2021-award-for-best-ceo-of-diversity.

power, resources, and support. Instead, you need to find a robust source of support at the top.

Be Curious to Make It Stick

A second point is that people often have strong reactions to the study of diversity. In fact, even the very word "diversity" is often reacted to with emotion. It makes some people anxious, others defensive, and still others angry. For this book to be the most digestible, it will be important for you to approach it with a neutral, curious perspective. Scrutinize it, yes. But try to approach it with an open mind. We will help you with that by presenting scientific facts and articles instead of opinions. Indeed, we are very science-minded researchers who have a total of more than 200 peer-reviewed, empirically based research publications. We present, in this book, many of these findings and other data-backed practices. We are not interested in the latest fads in diversity consulting; we do not opine on the use and meaning of the Implicit Associations Test; we are not advertising one particular consultant over another; and this is not a unified discussion of a single idea such as privilege or power, inclusive leadership, or racism. Instead, we are trying to make you aware of the research; how you can use empirically supported answers to try to improve the diversity-related issues in your organization; and how you can become a better, inclusive leader.

Similarly, apart from viewing diversity as an emotional topic, many people also view diversity as a political one. In fact, some political leaders have explicitly warned state agencies and public universities that some DEI programs are themselves illegal or discriminatory. We view diversity not as "a political" topic but as an "apolitical" one. We believe diversity should be important to everyone, regardless of your political affiliation, religion, or any other background characteristic. If you are part of a workplace organization, the topic of diversity is critical for you to understand and explore. This not just for those of you in human resources. It is not just for those of you who have a general interest in the area. And it is not just for top management. Rather, diversity is affecting all of us. Each of us has characteristics that make us different from others, and we live with people who are similar to us and different from us in other ways. We need to know how to best understand diversity and realize that it is a precious resource rather than an unfortunate circumstance that we "must manage." Still other people just do not know the facts and believe that diversity is more of an opinion-oriented topic. How you feel about diversity should not be the sum of an opinion devoid of facts that you stick to reverently. We write this book, then, with an intention to increase your understanding of DEI. We do this by amassing science.

Embrace Discomfort to Make It Stick

Another important point to convey is that many people admit that they want to talk about diversity but that they also feel incredibly unsure about what to say and how to say it. They are afraid and feel nervous, worried, guilty, judged, and/or unsafe expressing their authentic opinions, asking questions, becoming emotional, and making mistakes. This is hugely problematic because staying quiet may be the best way to ensure that status quo and disparities remain. In this book, we share the voices from the 50 members of a very diverse MBA class who willingly described their experiences. These individuals identified as female (26), Black (16), Hispanic (14), Asian (12), LGBTQ (7), first-generation college student (7), international (5), physically disabled (3), students/parents (3), immigrants (3), veterans (2), and Jewish (2). Each of these individuals is much more than any label, but throughout this book, we include some of their reflections and experiences.

One of these professionals (a Latina woman) reported that "I have always tried to work extra hard to prove myself, but I know that it shouldn't be the answer." Another member of the class (an Asian woman) communicated the urgency for organizations to attend to DEI by emphasizing that they should talk the talk and walk the walk. And soon. One of the biggest dangers that I see is talking too much about diversity and never taking clear action; the result is that employees start to become deaf to the messages and beliefs that change will never happen.

Daisy Auger-Dominguez,[5] Chief People Officer at Vice Media, provided some excellent suggestions about how to hold conversations about diversity. Auger-Dominguez argued that we can learn to ask better questions that amplify others' voices, remove barriers to their success, and contribute to the safe work environment that others experience. People can also educate themselves on the inequities that have existed since the birth of our country, the perspectives of marginalized individuals, and the compounding complexities that exist when people have intersectional identities. And people can lean into the uncomfortable feeling that each of us is, indeed, part of the problem. We can open up to the discomfort experienced by others who have been forced to be silenced. Finally, Auger-Dominguez argued that each of us needs to just start somewhere, even if it is only a small attempt to be more inclusive. If we are not being intentionally inclusive, we are probably being unintentionally exclusive. We need to read, listen, confront, and let allies know that they are very much needed.

These conversations about diversity, however uncomfortable they might be, are critical; such discourse can inspire action to help create stronger, better, and more inclusive organizations. Our hope is that by explaining the why and how of DEI with the science and stories shared in this book, we can encourage you to create space for more conversations on "working together."

---

[5] Auger-Dominguez, D. (2019, November 8). Getting over your fear of talking about diversity. Harvard Business Review.

SECTION 1
THE WHAT AND WHY OF WORKING TOGETHER

In 2022, New England Patriots coach Bill Belichick wrote a text message congratulating a man named Brian for landing the New York Giants head coaching position. There were two problems with this text. First, two people named Brian had upcoming interviews for the coaching position, and Coach Belichick texted the wrong Brian (he texted Brian Flores rather than Brian Daboll). Second, Brian Flores (a Black man with Honduran roots) had not even completed his interview for the position before the job was already promised to Brian Daboll (a White man). Flores filed a lawsuit against the National Football League (NFL) alleging racial discrimination in the hiring process. Flores argued that the interview was a sham, based only on the NFL's "Rooney Rule," which explicitly requires that at least one ethnic minority candidate be considered for coaching positions. This kind of "fake" interview was also apparently common at Wells Fargo, an organization that was also sued by job candidates from ethnic minority backgrounds.[1]

What is particularly notable about these cases is that both the NFL and Wells Fargo had created and implemented interview practices with the stated goal of increasing diversity. Hiring agents in both organizations knew they needed to include people from different racial backgrounds in the interview process. Yet they seem to have

---

[1] Flitter, E. (2022, May). At Wells Fargo, a quest to increase diversity led to fake interviews. *The New York Times*. https://www.nytimes.com/2022/05/19/business/wells-fargo-fake-interviews.html.

done so in a way that made it impossible for all candidates to have an equal chance at the jobs, and also in such a way that ultimately undermined the goal of diversity.

These cases exemplify some of the challenges facing individuals and organizations with regard to diversity, equity, and inclusion (DEI), and they underscore the need for clarifying what DEI are and why they matter. In this section, we define and describe the concepts of diversity, equity, and inclusion separately. In addition, we articulate three reasons why organizations should invest in DEI. We label them as imperatives and refer to them as (a) the realistic imperative, (b) the business imperative, and (c) the moral imperative.

1
What Is Diversity?

Even within the domain of professional sports, the ideals of diversity, equity, and inclusion (DEI) can represent a variety of people and circumstances; it is not just Black coaches in the National Football League who encounter inequity. One of the most successful female track and field athletes in Olympic history, Allyson Felix, faced a different kind of challenge off the track. Her sponsor, Nike, planned to slash her pay when she became pregnant. Recognizing her worth, and rejecting Nike's response, Felix joined with Athleta and the Women's Sports Foundation to continue competing and to address gender inequities in sports. One visible example of their work was the creation of grants to support athletes' competition childcare needs. Felix identified exclusionary aspects of athletics and is working to transform the environment for everyone. When announcing her last season on Instagram in 2022, she wrote, "This season I'm running for women. I'm running for a better future for my daughter. I'm running for you."

Brian Flores and Felix's experiences in professional sports reflect distinct but interconnected aspects of DEI. Given these complex processes and experiences, it is critical to ensure that we have a clear, consistent, and mutual understanding of what the terms "diversity" and "inclusion" actually mean.

There is no shortage of the ways in which people define diversity. The Cambridge Dictionary defines it as "the mixture of races and religions that make up a group of people." We think this definition is too narrow—diversity consists of more than just people of different races and religions. Clearly, it is the mixture of other groups of people, too, such as those varying in age, gender, abilities, and educational level. If dictionaries err on the side of being concise, let's turn to looking at definitions from inclusion offices whose job it is to study diversity.

The inclusion office at Virginia Commonwealth University defines diversity as "all the ways in which people differ, and it encompasses all the different characteristics that make one individual or group different from another." This definition is certainly more encompassing than the first one. The problem, however, is that this definition may be *too* exhaustive as to be helpful. There are limits to the types of diversity we are interested in examining—we are not interested in differences in the types of eyeglasses people decide to wear, individuals' shoe size, or what sorts of condiments people decide to squeeze into their sandwiches. Putting every possible variation in human condition, behavior, preference, or attitude into the definition of diversity begins to dilute the construct so much it renders it unhelpful.

We asked our MBA students to reflect on the identities and group memberships that shape their perspectives of diversity. Some of the words, phrases, and labels they shared include Asian woman, first-generation immigrant, military veteran, lawyer, Jewish, conservative, biracial, African, medical student, Latinx, Lebanese, bisexual, single, Christian, millennial, HBCU graduate, person with disability, and low-income background. One student shared that her identity does "not fit in the traditional boxes that we must complete for the census or job applications."

Scholars have tried to better conceptualize diversity by breaking it down into two different categories—surface-level and deep-level characteristics.[1] Surface-level characteristics involve often more readily visible characteristics that represent social categories such as gender, race and ethnicity, age, and some forms of disability. Surface-level characteristics might be particularly influential in determining organizational behaviors when people have limited a

---

[1] Harrison, D. A., Price, K. H., & Bell, M. P. (1998). Beyond relational demography: Time and the effects of surface- and deep-level diversity on work group cohesion. *Academy of Management Journal, 41*(1), 96–107.

priori knowledge of or past experiences with others who have one of these characteristics. In addition, these characteristics may matter more when people have very strong stereotypes and prejudices that they readily direct toward others who have the characteristics.

Deep-level characteristics involve aspects that are not typically immediately visible but over time come to substantially influence behaviors and social interactions. Deep-level characteristics include attitudes, opinions, and experiences—for example, religious preference, socioeconomic status, family-related status, sexual orientation, education level, military experience, communication style, and political affiliation.

The level differentiation can be useful in thinking about how the most rudimentary, often visible (e.g., surface-level) aspects of demography evoke different reactions than do those characteristics that emerge over time (e.g., deep-level). In this book, we focus on characteristics that come from both categories, although we concentrate mostly on social categories that have been tracked in a fairly comprehensible way over time by reputable, national polls.

For the purpose of this book and the action we hope to inspire, we consider *diversity* as the extent to which a group of people includes members that differ in socially meaningful ways from each other at work. This definition considers diversity to be a characteristic of groups or organizations, not individuals. This definition also is flexible enough to include many aspects of difference but intentionally does not include distinctions that may be less socially meaningful.

We further introduce *equity* as the existence of fair and just practices within organizations so that all members can thrive. It is a feeling that people are being treated fairly. Equity requires acknowledging that everyone does not start from the same place and adjustments are necessary for fairness. For instance, individuals who use wheelchairs should have access to meeting rooms that are wheelchair accessible; those who have hearing limitations should be able to access presentations that use closed captioning; and those holding workplace gatherings should consider dress codes (some people may not be able to afford or might not be able to wear certain clothes), meals that they are serving (some individuals have very substantial dietary restrictions), and the inclusion of and pressure to drink alcohol (some find this against their religious or moral beliefs).

In addition, we introduce and define *inclusion* as the process of ensuring that people from different backgrounds are invited to and appreciated in the workplace. This definition makes it clear why experts began referring to the study of diversity as the study of "diversity, equity, and inclusion." The addition of "inclusion" ensures that organizations do not just focus their attention only on recruiting, hiring, and/or promoting people from different backgrounds, or proverbially "getting their numbers up." Rather, organizations also need to ensure they are including and appreciating what people from diverse backgrounds bring to the organizations.

In "Diversity Doesn't Stick Without Inclusion,"[2] researchers suggested that organizations know how to quantify diversity but do not know how to define, measure, or encourage inclusiveness. Inclusion can be illustrated in organizations where people are encouraged to speak up and be heard, where it is safe for everyone to propose ideas and make decisions, where leaders take advice and give and implement feedback, and where team members are credited for successes. As diversity consultant Verna Myers succinctly stated, "Diversity is being invited to the party. Inclusion is being asked to dance." Equity might involve everyone getting the space they need on the dance floor. In short, then, if we bring the terms together, we have the culmination in DEI, which we could consider the process of including and valuing employees from different backgrounds.

We focus in this book on the broad concepts of DEI, but it is important to note that a number of other terms of these ideas are part of organizational discourse on these issues. Indeed, we shortchange the topic if we do not also define constructs closely related to diversity. Another related and important concept that has been raised by employees and captured by research is that of *authenticity*, or what we call the feeling that arises when employees feel safe enough to reveal their true and entire selves in the workplace. The authors

---

[2] Sherbin, L., & Rashid, R. (2017, February 1). Diversity doesn't stick without inclusion. *Harvard Business Review*.

of "Diversity and Authenticity"[3] argued that, often, marginalized employees are afraid to be their authentic selves in the workplace because some aspects of their true selves may not be understood, valued, or celebrated at work. Taking Verna Myers' party analogy further, we understand authenticity as being able to dance in the way and to the particular music you like.

Unfortunately, not many people report feeling like they can be very authentic in the workplace. In a 3,000-employee survey conducted from 20 different large U.S. firms, 61% of the employees believed they had to downplay their differences.[4] These employees were afraid they would not be fully accepted or would be penalized, so they "covered" in some way, or left the cane at work to hide a disability, used different pronouns to avoid discussing a same-sex boyfriend, changed their pattern of speech to sound "White," and avoided discussion of day care pickup to avoid a "motherhood penalty." Clearly, the study of DEI is not complete without consideration that its ultimate goal is to ensure that employees experience authenticity or the acceptance of who they truly are.[5]

DEI scholars and consultants have also emphasized the importance of belonging in organizations.[6] The need to belong—to be meaningfully connected to other people—is perhaps the most fundamental motivation in human life.[7] Psychological and physical well-being is inextricably linked with the extent to which people feel that they are part of enduring relationships. Yet, as much as 40% of employees feel that they are isolated at work.[8] Helping people feel that they belong may be a critical component of effective DEI efforts.

---

[3] Phillips, K. W., Dumas, T. L., & Rothbard, N. P. (2018, March–April). Diversity and authenticity. *Harvard Business Review*.

[4] Yoshino, K., & Smith, C. (2014, March). Fear of being different stifles talent. *Harvard Business Review*.

[5] Cook, K. S., & Hegtvedt, K. A. (1983). Distributive justice, equity, and equality. *Annual Review of Sociology, 9*(1), 217–241.

[6] Shore, L. M., Randel, A. E., Chung, B. G., Dean, M. A., Holcombe Ehrhart, K., & Singh, G. (2011). Inclusion and diversity in work groups: A review and model for future research. *Journal of Management, 37*(4), 1262–1289.

[7] Baumeister, R. F., & Leary, M. R. (1995). The need to belong: Desire for interpersonal attachments as a fundamental human motivation. *Psychological Bulletin, 117*(3), 497–529.

[8] Carr, E. W., Reece, A., Kellerman, G. R., & Robichaux, A. (2019, December 16). The value of belonging at work. *Harvard Business Review*.

It is not surprising that many employees question whether they should attempt to cover or downplay their identities. Indeed, the United States traditionally has been referred to as a melting pot in which generations of people from different countries and backgrounds have come together to become a single, blended society. The idea was to blend, and that meant stigmatized people tried to downplay or hide their differences. It was common for people to try to stop speaking non-English languages and rid themselves of accents revealing their original homeland. Similarly, immigrants ceased celebrating ethnic cultural practices that would make them look different from others. In short, the goal was to meld together following established, dominant norms and not appear different.

Other times, people have used a different metaphor. And this is the notion of an ingredient-laden salad. This metaphor represents the idea that people from diverse backgrounds can live together in harmony without giving up their uniqueness. Furthermore, the dressing might be thought of as the common ingredient. So, being American is the common ingredient, but people come from and represent many different backgrounds.

These metaphors have different consequences for the workplace. If employees endorse a "melting pot" view, they do not need to discuss the characteristics they hold that make them diverse.[9] Rather, they can check their identity at the door and organizations will protect them. In this view, the organization need not take an individually tailored approach to meeting employees' differing needs. However, if instead employees hold a "salad" view, they may be more likely to believe that diversity is critical for producing the best outcomes in organizations. Such employees would be interested in working for organizations where they not only feel included but also feel like they can be their authentic selves. Another consequence of this view is the stifling of innovation and full participation in the workplace when employees hide or code-switch in order to assimilate to the norms of the dominant culture.

---

[9] Twaronite, K. (2019, February 28). The surprising power of simply asking coworkers how they're doing. *Harvard Business Review*.

Tools for Working Together

Reflect on the following questions about your current or most recent organization:

1. Are different racial/ethnic groups or women more represented at the lower levels of your organization? Are White men overrepresented in upper levels of leadership?
2. Consider the difference between surface- and Deep-level diversity. When you focus on diversity, do you tend to focus on surface-level characteristics that are more visible and salient? Why might deep-level characteristics be equally important to consider?
3. How is inclusion different from the mere representation of diversity in an organization? Does your organization have adequate representation? Does it go beyond basic inclusion to also adopt policies and practices that facilitate inclusion and authenticity from diverse group members?
4. Consider the metaphors of the melting pots versus salad bowl. Which metaphor does your company adopt? Are people in your organization discouraged from being authentic and expected to downplay aspects of their diverse identities (examples of the melting pot metaphor)? Or are they encouraged to embrace their authentic expression, inclusion, and have their unique experiences/backgrounds valued (examples of the salad bowl metaphor)?

2

The Realistic Imperative of Diversity

Approximately 10 years ago, something unprecedented began happening in birthing wards throughout America. A big change. And it was a change that one of the authors of this book experienced for herself. After giving birth to a very pale-skin, red-headed baby, Mikki went to look for him in the nursery. He was easy to spot. There baby Jackson was, lying in his bassinet among a sea of other bassinets containing dark-haired (or bald!) beautiful babies who had a variety of different skin tones, all of which were considerably darker. Yes, since 2011, more minority babies have been born in the United States than White babies. And this trend is expected to continue for the foreseeable future and will have a very tremendous long-term impact on our society and on our workplaces.

This reality of demographic change is the first reason that organizations should invest in diversity. Indeed, there are some very dramatic changes that have already and are continuing to take place in the U.S. population. These changes have happened, are happening, and will continue to happen. They portend seismic shifts in the workforce that will continue to unfold for the foreseeable next quarter of a century. In this chapter, we discuss these changing demographics. We summarize the most significant population changes and consider how they have and/or will impact the workforce.[1] The evidence used draws heavily from the national authorities on demography—the U.S. Census Bureau, the U.S. Bureau of Labor Statistics, and the

---

[1] Toosi, M. (2016, September). *A look at the future of the U.S. labor force to 2060*. U.S. Bureau of Labor Statistics. https://www.bls.gov/spotlight/2016/a-look-at-the-future-of-the-us-labor-force-to-2060/home.htm.

Pew Research Center. These sources examine the workforce, defined as non-institutional (e.g., not in prison or mental health facilities) civilians (i.e., not in the Armed Forces) who are 16 years of age or older and employed or actively seeking employment. They typically use population projections produced by the U.S. Census Bureau, which reports trends in births, deaths, and immigration and also trends in workforce participation for a number of demographic groups.

In describing the reality of the U.S. population and labor force, we draw organizational members' attention to these realities. We believe that many organizations have not responded appropriately to some of these demographic changes that already have happened. We need organizations to understand the reality of these numbers because a very significant portion of the success of U.S. organizations is predicated on their solid understanding of these continuing, anticipated changes and the way in which they prepare and adapt to them.

Declining Population Growth

The population growth rate is slowing down. In fact, the U.S. Census Bureau reveals that the U.S. population grew only 0.16% during the first full pandemic year of 2020–21, which marks the slowest rate since the Great Depression in 1937. This decreased rate is the function of at least two major factors. First, the U.S. birth rate is decreasing. In 2020, the number of babies born in the United States fell to the lowest point since 1979.[2] Many women are choosing to have fewer children or choosing to forego having them at all. In addition, the rates of teenage pregnancies and unintentional pregnancies have declined, likely due to an increase in availability and use of contraception. Similar birth rates are expected to continue during the next 50 years.

---

[2] Osterman, M. J., Hamilton, B. E., Martin, J. A., Driscoll, A. K., & Valenzuela, C. P. (2023). National Vital Statistics Reports. *National Vital Statistics Reports, 72*(1), 1–52.

Second, the United States has begun observing a historic number of deaths every year, and this trend is expected to continue as a larger number of baby boomers continue to age. The baby boomers, or people who were born between 1946 and 1964, currently represent approximately 29% of the population. By 2030, however, all baby boomers will be older than age 65 years. Between 2030 and 2050, most of the baby boomers will die and a significant share of the U.S. population will be lost. A gaming platform, Incendar, even tracks (i.e., search "baby boomer death clock") the ongoing, real-time loss of this important generation. At the same time, millennials, or people who were born between 1981 and 1996, are projected to soon take over the baby boomers as the largest generation in the United States.

During the next 50 years, these two trends leading to a decreasing population growth rate will have a very significant impact on the workforce. Fewer younger people will be entering the workforce because they are choosing to invest in their education and stay in school longer. While the workforce will be aged in an unprecedented way, there also will be a very significant number of people (particularly those who are older) who retire. One result of these projected trends is that immigration from certain areas (e.g., Asia) will make up for the otherwise precipitous decline.

An Aging Workforce

Despite the fact that millennials will soon comprise the largest generation, the projections show that the average age of the general population is higher than ever and will continue to rise for a while. In 2017, the U.S. Census Bureau predicted that by 2030, one in every five residents will be aged 65 years or older. During this time, a milestone will be reached such that older people will be projected to outnumber children for the first time in U.S. history. In 2018, the U.S. Census Bureau projected that there will be 78.0 million people in 2035 and 88.5 million by 2050 who are aged 65 years or older.

As a result of the aging population, the average age of employees in the U.S. workforce is increasing because many older people are choosing to stay in the workforce longer. Before Congress amended the Age Discrimination in Employment Act, people could be forced to retire when they reached age 65 years. That is no longer the case except in a few occupations deemed particularly perilous or demanding (e.g., air traffic controllers, pilots, military, and law enforcement). Hence, people are able to work longer and are deciding to do this because they want to stay busy, they enjoy their jobs, and/or they need financial security.

As a result of the aging population, there is also a very real need for an increased understanding of work–family stressors. Because the population is aging, job growth in the health care sector is expected to increase. Simply stated, many more people are getting older, and many more people will need the health care associated with aging. But much of the needed care will come from children or grandchildren, who will need to balance their jobs with the part-time or full-time care of one or more parents or grandparents. Organizations need to consider how they are going to manage this exponentially growing problem that their employees are going to face.

Women in the Workplace

The growth rates of women (and men[3]) in the workforce are expected to decrease. For almost two decades, the participation rate of women in the workforce increased, from 50.9% in 1979 to a high of 60% in 1999. Since then, however, the overall rate has been slightly declining and is expected to continue to do so until it reaches 51.9% in 2060. However, the COVID-19 pandemic was certainly a game changer for these predictions, given the substantial increases in labor force exits, particularly for non-White women and women

---

[3] We could not find any research on the growth in workforce participation rates for nonbinary individuals.

with children younger than age 6 years.[4] Of course, the workforce participation rate for men has also been decreasing, steadily declining from 77.8% in 1979 to 74.7% in 1999, and it is projected to be 62.3% in 2060.

Perhaps a bigger issue with women in the workplace is that so many organizations have not succeeded in systematically treating female employees equally with their male counterparts. Currently, there continues to be a very substantial pay gap between the genders, in which women make 80 cents to every dollar a man makes. Women do not experience the same advancement to leadership opportunities as do men. Women are not well represented on boards of publicly traded companies. There is a large imbalance of firms that have male but not female co-owners and top managers. Women do not tend to be positioned at the executive, more prestigious, and financially lucrative positions. In fact, an article published in *The New York Times* in 2018 pointed out that of chief executive officers (CEOs) in the *Fortune* 500 companies, there were more men named James, John, Robert, or William who were CEOs than there were all women as a whole.[5] As of 2023, the number of female CEOs of *Fortune* 500 companies had risen from 24 (4.8%) to an all-time high of 53 (10.4%). However, if U.S. society is going to get serious about utilizing the talent that women can provide, organizations are going to need to adopt all the steps necessary to ensure that there are no gender differences in the rates at which employees are hired, valued, developed, promoted, reinforced, and treated equally.

---

[4] Lim, K., & Zabek, M. (2021, October). *Women's labor force exits during COVID-19: Differences by motherhood, race, and ethnicity.* Federal Reserve Board. https://www.federalreserve.gov/econres/feds/womens-labor-force-exits-during-covid-19-differences-by-motherhood-race-and-ethnicity.htm.

[5] Miller, C. C., Quealy, K., & Sanger-Katz, M. (2018, April 24). The top jobs where women are outnumbered by men named John. *The New York Times.*

Pregnant Women, Mothers, and New Parents in the Workplace

One of the reasons that the participation rate for women may be decreasing over time is a continued lack of support for mothers. This often makes it infeasible for both parents to work because of the high costs of child care, burdens on the family, and lack of working incentives. Yet, our future will see more pregnant women in the workplace than ever before. Currently, 5% of women in the workforce are pregnant at any given time, but this percentage is expected to rise. This is not because there are more pregnancies; rather, it is because data suggest up to 72% of employees who get pregnant now continue to work until they are at least 6 months pregnant, with many increasingly working until the final month or their actual deliveries. Furthermore, the majority of women return only a few weeks following birth. Organizations have been slow to address the issues facing pregnant women. For instance, the United States remains the only industrialized country that does not provide mothers (or fathers) universal paid family leave. This partially accounts for the United States being rated so low as a country (43rd out of 146 countries in 2023) on gender equity by the World Economic Forum.[6] However, the District of Columbia and 11 states—California, Colorado, Connecticut, Delaware, Maryland, Massachusetts, New Jersey, New York, Oregon, Rhode Island, and Washington—have mandated paid family leave, and many organizations are leading the way in giving mothers (and parents) what they want and deserve, namely paid time off with their newborn babies.

Racial and Immigrant Makeup

Although non-Hispanic White people are the largest racial group in the overall population (60% in 2023), they are estimated to comprise only 46% of the population by 2065. The Hispanic population in the

---

[6] https://www.weforum.org/publications/global-gender-gap-report-2023

United States is moving in the other direction and will particularly shape the future demographics of the country. There were a record 59.9 million U.S. Latino people (18.7% of the population) in 2023, and this group is expected to comprise 24% of the population by 2065. Asian people comprised 7% of the U.S. population in 2023, and this group is anticipated to double (14%) by 2065. The percentage of Black people is anticipated to remain fairly steady, increasing from 12% of the population in 2023 to 13% by 2065.

The trends in the racial composition of the U.S. workforce are anticipated to mirror the projected population changes—in particular, the Hispanic percentage of the labor force is expected to increase more than that of any other group by 2026. This is not reflective of the projected immigration of Hispanic people to the United States (in fact, this is expected to sharply decline) but, rather, due to the large number of young Hispanic people already in the country. In 2023, the median age of U.S.-born Hispanic people was 21 years, an age at which they have already or will soon join the workforce.[7]

The substantial increase in Asian employees into the workforce is expected largely due to immigration. In fact, the number of Asian immigrants is expected to increase more than any other group. Because Asian immigrants tend to be better educated than other immigrants, the overall education level of immigrants is also likely to rise. It is important to note, however, that the actual immigration rates will depend on the future governments and the immigration policies they create and enforce.

Religious Preferences

Christianity will continue to predominate as the most common religious preference in the U.S. population; however, the projected population of Christian people is expected to decrease during the next 30 years. Specifically, the Pew Research Center projects that

---

[7] Moslimani, M., Lopez, M. H., & Noe-Bustamante, L. (2023, August 16). 11 facts about Hispanic origin groups in the U.S. Pew Research Center.

the 78.3% of the U.S. population affiliated as Christian in 2010 will decrease to 66.4% by 2050. To a large extent, this decrease will be supplanted with an increase in the number of people who do not affiliate with any particular religion (from 16.4% to 25.6%). But the change will also be influenced by the growing number of Muslim people (from 0.9% to 2.1%). By 2040, Muslims are expected to be the second largest religious group in the United States, and it is anticipated that there will be 8.1 million Muslim affiliates by 2050. This is more than a doubling of the current Muslim population in the United States. As such, we need to make sure they are fully welcomed and included in the workforce.

Disability in the Workforce

According to the U.S. Bureau of Labor Statistics, 21% of people with a disability of working age are employed, signifying the highest ever recorded rate.[8] Evenso, this statistic is far lower than the 65.4% of nondisabled individuals without disabilities who are working.[9] Yet, the number of disabled individuals in the workforce is gradually increasing. And given that the likelihood of disability status increases with age, a much larger increase in disabled employees engaging in the workforce is expected. Continued developments in technology, greater use of remote and flexible working arrangements, and the reduction of damaging stereotypes pave the way for a future in which a greater percentage of individuals who possess disabilities enter the workforce.

---

[8] U.S. Bureau of Labor Statistics (2023, February 28). Employment–population ratio for people with a disability increases to 21.3 percent in 2022. https://www.bls.gov/opub/ted/2023/employment-population-ratio-for-people-with-a-disability-increases-to-21-3-percent-in-2022

[9] U.S. Bureau of Labor Statistics (2023, February 28). Employment–population ratio for people with a disability increases to 21.3 percent in 2022. https://www.bls.gov/opub/ted/2023/employment-population-ratio-for-people-with-a-disability-increases-to-21-3-percent-in-2022

Sexuality and Gender Identity

Many organizations can still improve the ways that they support LGBTQ+ employees. Because these identities can be invisible, it is difficult to get an accurate count of what the current and/or future percentage of LGBT individuals is not only in the U.S. population but also in the U.S. workforce. People who report being LGBTQ+ comprise 4.5% of the population, although polls suggest that people generally perceive estimates that are five times as high. This discrepancy is likely due, at least in part, to the fact that until recently, the United States had very inconsistent laws prohibiting discrimination in the workplace on the basis of sexual orientation or gender identity. Thus, many LGBTQ employees remained "closeted" and were afraid to disclose their sexual orientation or gender identity. At the federal level, in June 2020, the Supreme Court affirmed the *Bostock v. Clayton County, Georgia*[10] decision, clarifying that federal laws prohibiting employment discrimination based on sex apply to LGBTQ discrimination. This was a colossal victory for LGBTQ+ employees. However, the recent *Dobbs* ruling restricting women from reproductive freedom shows how permeable such basic rights can be, and recent comments from Supreme Court Justice Clarence Thomas suggest he invites future legal challenges regarding the marriage rights for LGBTQ individuals.[11]

A Bifurcation in Education Levels

In general, the workforce of the future will be more highly educated. More young people than ever are deciding to stay in secondary school and get at least some college credits, a phenomenon that is also driving up the average age of the workforce. Whereas less than half of the workforce had some education beyond high school in

---

[10] *Bostock v. Clayton County, Georgia*. 140 S.Ct. 1731 (2020), Nos. 17-1618, 17-1623, 18-107.
[11] Barragan, J. (2022, June 24). In Roe decision, Justice Clarence Thomas invites new legal challenges to contraception and same-sex marriage rights. *The Texas Tribune*. https://www.texastribune.org/2022/06/24/roe-wade-clarence-thomas-contraception-same-sex-marriage.

2005, almost two-thirds of them are expected to achieve some education beyond a high school diploma in 2025. The significant number of anticipated immigrants, particularly from Asia, are also expected to be very well-educated.

Although the workforce as a whole will be more educated, staggering differences will arise as a function of the predicted educational levels that White versus non-White people obtain. And race strongly interacts with education to create very different workplace outcomes. The majority of the workforce will no longer be White by 2032. The majority (two-thirds) of these non-White people will not have a college degree, referred to as the working class. This means that there will be major economic inequality between non-White people in working-class positions and White people in higher level positions. Immigrants (largely Asian) who enter the workforce will help fill many roles in which high levels of education are needed, but this means that Hispanic and Black individuals will see a very different set of workplace paygrades and opportunities than will White (and Asian) people.

Related to these educational differences, then, is the construct of differences in socioeconomic status (SES), which refers to a combined measure of an individual's economic and social work experience and ability to access resources relative to others. In calculating SES, one typically examines household income, educational levels, and occupations. This construct allows one to assess a measure of how much income and resources individuals have relative to the balance of how much they financially need, and it is also sometimes referred to more commonly as social class. Scientists are beginning to recognize that more research needs to be done to understand the very sizable influence that SES has on health and wellbeing.[12] Similarly, organizations should also be taking note and realizing that almost everyone believes their social class influences their work experiences in some way. For instance, it may influence perceptions of fit (how well employers believe they will excel at a

---

[12] Williams, J. C., Multhaup, M., & Mihaylo, S. (2018, September 5). Why companies should add class to their diversity discussions. *Harvard Business Review*.

job or in a particular organization) or knowledge of unspoken rules (e.g., navigating communication, wearing proper attire, following the chain of command, use caution in questioning your boss).

As a whole, the demographic changes in the workforce mean that organizations of the future will be different from those of today and yesterday. Organizations that want to be competitive must adapt. They need to become aware of the changing demographics so that these demographics can be better addressed. Workplace diversity is unavoidable. These projections, coupled with growing recognition of the importance of multiple or intersecting identities, convey the certainty of diversity in organizations. And this change is here, whether organizations are ready for it or not.

Tools for Working Together

1. Reflect on your family and friends and consider the following questions: Is your extended family more diverse than it was one or two generations ago? How so? In what ways have you personally witnessed the changing demographics in your friendship groups, neighborhood, and other social groups?
2. Think about your experiences at work and consider the following questions: How do you personally feel about differences or working with people who are different from you? Do you notice others' differences?
3. Consider your views on diversity more broadly: What are they? Do you think reflecting on your views about diversity can help you work with others who are different? How might this help?
4. Think about various kinds of diversity within your workplace: In what ways are the changing demographics of the workforce reflected at your organization? Are the broad categories of diversity represented or missing at your organization? Is the diversity diffused throughout the organization (across both divisions and levels of authority)?

3
The Financial Imperative of Diversity

In 2022, Walmart created a celebration edition Juneteenth ice cream brand to commemorate Juneteenth National Independence Day, which was designated as a federal holiday in June 2021. The Walmart ice cream had a printed statement on the carton that read, "Share and celebrate African-American culture, emancipation, and enduring hope." Backlash ensued. Critics argued that Walmart was commercializing, engaging in cultural appropriation, and making light of an event that marked the end of slavery. In addition, the flavor—a red-velvet swirl and cheesecake—was almost identical to another Black-owned brand, Creamalicious. Walmart pulled the product only a few weeks after its release. Marketing mistakes such as these can lead to widespread consumer avoidance of the product: associated firms can become the target of humiliation and stigma, which can result in millions of dollars of lost revenue. Many of these problems can be avoided by employing multicultural, multinational, and/or multilingual people to create, review, and implement marketing campaigns.

There are at least three arguments behind the business case for diversity. First, organizational diversity is a business advantage. By understanding the changing demographics, organizations can understand new forms of purchasing power, develop and market products toward diverse clientele, and harness diversity to prevent product errors. Second, discrimination is costly, and diversity helps prevent costs incurred due to discrimination. Organizations lose billions of dollars in discrimination claims and lawsuits, most of which are entirely preventable. Third, diversity in teams can be positively linked with job-related outcomes. Although diversity can be challenging, diversity in organizations can be linked to a number of positive outcomes, including increased innovation, creativity, and more accurate decision-making.

Diversity in Organizations Can Create a Business Advantage

Approximately 80% of organizations use the business case to describe the importance of diversity.[1] And why not? The consulting giant McKinsey commissioned one of the most well-cited studies showing that organizational diversity is beneficial for firm performance. McKinsey compared earnings in organizations that had the most gender diversity (the top quartile) with organizations with the least gender diversity (the bottom quartile). Its analyses suggested that the most gender diverse organizations tended to outperform those with little diversity, and they also outperformed the national average by 15%. Moreover, when analysts at McKinsey compared the top and bottom quartiles of organizations with respect to racial diversity, they found even greater differences. Companies in the top quartile for racial diversity were 35% more likely to outperform national industry means. Although these patterns were replicated again in 2018 and 2020, the replicability of these is tempered by Hand and Green's examination of similar data.[2,3]

Understanding and responding to the diverse perspectives of stakeholders can give organizations a competitive advantage for a number of reasons. We describe several of these:

---

[1] Georgeac, O., & Rattan, A. (2022, June 15). Stop making the business case for diversity. *Harvard Business Review*.
[2] Green, J., & Hand, J. R. M. (2021, August 6). Diversity matters/delivers/wins revisited in S&P 500® firms. SSRN. https://ssrn.com/abstract=3849562.
[3] Todd, S. (2021, July 29). Is McKinsey wrong about the financial benefits of diversity? *Quartz at Work*. https://qz.com/work/2038103/is-mckinsey-wrong-about-the-financial-benefits-of-diversity.

Changing demographics suggest future trends in purchasing power: The demographic shifts in the population also signify future shifts in purchasing power and consumer trends.[4] Fewer people may mean fewer people buying products. A decrease in the middle-class may mean more top and lower store catering. Older people may mean important business opportunities in health care, driverless vehicles, online shipping, more phones, and fewer vehicles. More people from Latinx or Asian backgrounds may mean attention to differences in food, entertainment, and lifestyle could benefit business.

New product development and success: Enhancing diversity through product inclusion in an organization typically increases product development and success.[5] Companies that have had increases in new product development and success include Mary Kay, Rent the Runway, Stitchfix, Barbie, Spanx, Black Entertainment Television, Ellevest Investing—all of which were created by people of color or [White] women understanding and reflectively what people of color or [White] women respectively often want or need. When people from a variety of backgrounds are represented in organizations, stakeholders from a variety of backgrounds may ultimately be served better.

Reducing advertising failures: Marketing campaigns to create brand awareness and buy-in can lead to dramatic increases in sales, but they can also lead to poor revenue and company embarrassment if companies do not invest in a diverse workforce. Consider, for instance, that the Scandinavian vacuum company Electrolux used the slogan "Nothing Sucks Like an Electrolux," in which "sucks" refers (in Swedish) to the substantial suction; in the United States, however, "sucks" obviously refers

---

[4] University of Georgia. (2021, August 11). Consuming buying power is more diverse than ever. *Newswise*. https://www.newswise.com/articles/consumer-buying-power-is-more-diverse-than-ever.

[5] Jean-Baptiste, A. (2020). *Building for everyone: Expand your market with design practices from Google's product inclusion team*. Wiley.

to a product not many people would want.[6] When Kentucky Fried Chicken began opening doors in China, it misstepped by translating its slogan "finger-licking good" into "eat your fingers off."[7] And when Pepsi began advertising in China, its slogan "Come alive with Pepsi" translated to "Pepsi brings your ancestors back from the dead."

Reducing product failures: Ensuring diverse perspectives are at the table can also create a business advantage by reducing product failures. Without diverse perspectives and experiences in designing and testing, products and their advertisements can fail users from systematically minoritized social groups. The first airbags to be installed in vehicles failed to protect women because they were tested with male crash dummies who did not have female anatomy. The first voice recognition programs did not recognize female voices and many accents because the programs were built and tested by men and native English speakers. An internet search browser's photo image recognition software labeled two Black individuals as gorillas. In 2014, Apple launched Apple Health, an application to monitor what Apple's Vice President of Software Engineering called "all of your metrics that you're most interested in." The application tracked some of what Apple considered to be the most important metrics (e.g., lab results, sodium intake, blood sugar, and cholesterol), but it did not track menstruation.[8] One industry that has had a consistent number of setbacks related to a lack of first obtaining perspectives of or reactions from a diverse set of employees is the fashion industry. As *Vogue Business* reports,[9]

---

[6] Absolute Translations. (2019, August 23). *Marketing fails caused by language barriers.* https://www.absolutetranslations.com/2019/08/23/marketing-fails-caused-by-language-barriers.

[7] Schooley, S. (2021, November 1). Lost in translation: 10 international marketing failure. *Business News Daily.* https://www.businessnewsdaily.com/5241-international-marketing-fails.html.

[8] Eveleth, R. (2014, December 15). How self-tracking apps exclude women. *The Atlantic.* https://www.theatlantic.com/technology/archive/2014/12/how-self-tracking-apps-exclude-women/383565/.

[9] Binkley, C. (2019, April, 30). Fashion's lack of diversity has real costs. *Vogue Business.* https://www.voguebusiness.com/companies/fashion-diversity-councils-innovation-revenue.

Gucci and Prada "had to pull products off shelves that evoked blackface," and Burberry used a noose on the runway. It further reports that the implications can be enormous, suggesting that Dolce & Gabbana's brand health in China decreased following the use of ads that insulted Chinese women.

Reducing communication failures: Ensuring diversity in employees and the languages they speak can also help reduce failures associated with communication errors. A study published in *JAMA Pediatrics*[10] showed that families with limited comfort in speaking English were twice as likely to have hospitalized children who experienced medical errors. Of the 147 families studied, 17.7% of those with limited English versus 9.6% of those comfortable with English reported medical errors that ranged from incorrect medical dosing to allergic reactions to drugs from a known allergy. Providing such diversity in languages is important as the United States continues to become more diverse; currently, throughout the country, approximately 50 languages other than English are commonly spoken between health care providers and their patients.[11] A similar set of communication errors occurs when non-English speakers receive medication with drug labels that are not translated. In many states, there are very limited laws in place to ensure the existence of free translation services for patients who need or request language translation on such prescriptions. Moreover, even computer-generated English-to-Spanish translation instructions result in inconsistent and potentially hazardous translations.[12]

---

[10] Khan, A., Yin, H. S., Brach, C., Graham, D. A., Ramotar, M. W., Williams, D. N., Spector, N., Landrigan, C. P., & Dreyer, B. P. (2020, October 19). Association between parent comfort with English and adverse events among hospitalized children. *JAMA Pediatrics, 174*(12), e203215. doi:10.1001/jamapediatrics.2020.3215.

[11] AMN Healthcare. (2021, August 25). *A world language index: A national and state-by-state listing of the most frequently spoken languages other than English in hospital, medical group and community health center-based patient encounters* [White paper]. https://www.amnhealthcare.com/amn-insights/whitepapers/healthcare-world-language-index.

[12] Sharif, I., & Tse, J. (2010). Accuracy of computer-generated, Spanish-language medicine labels. *Pediatrics, 125*(5), 960–965. https://doi.org/10.1542/peds.2009-2530.

The potential impact of organizational diversity in providing a business advantage may sometimes seem relatively minor—designs that fail to ensure that shorter people (often women) can reach a kitchen shelf or overhead bin on an airplane can easily be remedied by a step stool or a helping hand. But why not design them adequately from the start? And some issues are much more weighty—when body armor and airbags are designed to be equally effective for people with a range of body types but are not in actuality, more serious consequences emerge.

Diversity Can Lead to Lower Levels of Discrimination

There is a financial imperative for diversity because its absence is often either a result or an antecedent of discrimination. And discrimination can be very costly. Estimates suggest that discrimination costs $64 billion annually. One source of these costs is litigation related to formal claims of workplace discrimination, which costs employers a significant sum. A jury awarded $125 million for compensatory and punitive damages to a plaintiff in a 2021 disability discrimination case against Walmart.[13] In this case, the plaintiff was a former employee with Down syndrome who was fired after absences she said resulted from a lack of accommodations to meet the transportation needs dictated by her disability. The jury's verdict indicated not only that she suffered from lost pay ($150,000 in compensatory damages) but also that the jury believed the plaintiff had been treated egregiously ($125 million in punitive damages).

Another source of these costs is employee turnover; approximately 2 million employees leave their jobs due to discrimination.[14]

---

[13] U.S. Equal Employment Opportunity Commission. (2021, July 16). *Jury awards over $125 million in EEOC disability discrimination case against Walmart* [Press Release]. https://www.eeoc.gov/newsroom/jury-awards-over-125-million-eeoc-disability-discrimination-case-against-walmart.

[14] Burns, C. (2012, March 22). *The costly business of discrimination.* Center for American Progress. https://www.americanprogress.org/article/the-costly-business-of-discrimination.

This is hugely problematic given that recruiting, onboarding, and training a new employee can cost exorbitant amounts that often exceed an employee's annual salary. In addition, turnover can result in reduced team or company morale, increased stress, and a risk of legal claims. Even if employees are not leaving their jobs altogether, estimates suggest that discrimination results in increased employee absence that amounts to a substantial amount in lost productivity.

In addition to the costs of discrimination, there are costs of lost opportunity. Talent management decisions across the talent management cycle, from selection to development to compensation, that are based on job-irrelevant characteristics can result in a lower quality workforce with less ability to generate profits. If organizations are failing to hire or promote diverse talent, they are making poor business decisions.

Diversity in Teams Can Lead to Favorable Outcomes

Team diversity can be positively associated with a number of outcomes, such as greater innovation and improved decision-making. Indeed, diverse teams can be more innovative than homogeneous teams.[15] When we are in a homogeneous group, we all tend to be thinking the same way, with similar strategies, with the same tool set and experience to draw upon. To promote innovation, we should include people who look at things very differently and who have different ways of thinking about, interacting with, and reacting to the world. Kathy Phillips[16] examined decades of research on innovation and found that people with different backgrounds bring different information, new opinions, and new perspectives. Therefore,

---

[15] Talke, K., Salomo, S., & Kock, A. (2011). Top management team diversity and strategic innovation orientation: The relationship and consequences for innovativeness and performance. *Journal of Product Innovation Management, 28*(6), 819–832. https://doi.org/10.1111/j.1540-5885.2011.00851.x

[16] Phillips, K. (2014, October 1). How diversity makes us smarter. *Scientific American.* https://www.scientificamerican.com/article/how-diversity-makes-us-smarter.

unsurprisingly, companies with more diverse leadership teams reported higher innovation revenues: 45% versus 26%.

Data suggest that diverse groups are more likely to ask questions than homogeneous teams, and they show fewer inaccuracies in the decisions they make because they spend more time considering and discussing issues.

But It's Complicated

Before we end this chapter on the financial advantages of diversity, we feel compelled to talk about one of the enormous drawbacks of this framing. While people—particularly many business leaders—often love to hear about the bottom line and might favor this approach for its focus on savings and losses, we also recognize it is overly simplistic and potentially offensive. Researchers Robin Ely and David Thomas, who have been studying diversity for decades, concluded that a *simplistic* business case for diversity is not that persuasive.[17] They claim that often people think adding diversity alone will automatically increase organizational effectiveness; however, increased effectiveness only emerges when organizations are able to harness the diversity and reshape the power structures within them. In order to make diversity work, Ely and Thomas[18] argue that organizations must (a) build trust or an environment in which people feel safe; (b) get leaders to understand how oppression and privilege operate in the larger context, identify it in their own organization; and root it out; (c) embrace a wide range of style and voices rather than just that of the prototypical White man; and (d) make cultural differences a resource for learning and innovation.

There are additional problems that can occur when organizations focus too narrowly and exclusively on the business case: It commoditizes people from marginalized backgrounds, focuses too narrowly on profit,

---

[17] Ely, R. J., & Thomas, D. A. (2020, November–December). Getting serious about diversity: Enough already with the business case. *Harvard Business Review*.
[18] Ely, R. J., & Thomas, D. A. (2020, November–December). Getting serious about diversity: Enough already with the business case. *Harvard Business Review*.

forgets about the arguments for justice and fairness, and leads to backlash when organizations experience diversity-related challenges.[19,20] When our class of MBA students was asked about how they respond to the business or financial case for diversity, some indicated the limitations of the business case, expressing, "I react negatively. While I know the business case is solid and exists, it feels like there should not need to be some monetary incentive attached in order for business leaders to recognize and support our humanity" and, similarly, that

> It is too simplistic or myopic to say that there is a business case for diversity. Diversity should be a status quo because we are humans and equal. We should all have the same potential for success (regardless of a business' bottom line).

These reactions suggest that it might be best to avoid emphasizing the business case. In their article titled "Stop Making the Business Case for Diversity,"[21] Georgia and Rattan agree, revealing that the business case (vs. an emphasis on a moral case or no case at all) leads employees from minoritized backgrounds to feel less belongingness with the company and to be more concerned about being stereotyped, and they are more likely to be seen interchangeably with other members of their group.

Tools for Working Together

Consider the following reflection questions:

1. To whom do you think the "business case" for diversity speaks to most loudly? Why is the financial imperative the business perspective?

---

[19] McCloskey, H. N. (2020, August 3). *Stop making the business case for diversity*. Sifted. https://sifted.eu/articles/diversity-business-case.
[20] Zheng, L. (2019, July 24). *The business case for diversity is a sinking ship*. https://lilyzheng.co/the-business-case-for-diversity-is-a-sinking-ship.
[21] Georgeac, O., & Rattan, A. (2022, June 15). Stop making the business case for diversity. *Harvard Business Review*.

2. What are the drawbacks to focusing predominantly or only on the financial imperative or bottom line of diversity?
3. How can we prevent organizations from commodifying people from marginalized or minoritized backgrounds?
4. Can you think of any examples in your own past or current organization in which failures may have occurred and/or been reduced with the consideration of more diverse perspectives?

4
The Moral Imperative of Diversity

After an invitation to a 5-day leadership retreat in the high mountains of Colorado, Mikki realized she had no appropriate gear for backpacking and camping. The distributed packing list was extensive; however, a guide recommended she could get most of it at Patagonia. Surfing the website, she quickly fell in love with the products. Of course! Who wouldn't dream of a luxury night of mountain sleeping with a Patagonia Macro Puff Quilt[1] with "revolutionary lightweight PlumaFill insulation" and an "ultralight nylon ripstop PertexR Quantum shell," which "is water-resistant, windproof and treated with a DWR (durable water repellant) finish." (Really, who thinks of all this?)

What gained Mikki's attention even more was the very surprising depictions of the Patagonia company. Since its inception in 1973, it has practiced corporate social responsibility (CSR), otherwise known as a set of policies and practices that are intended to be socially accountable to itself, its customers, its stakeholders, and the world at large. For Patagonia, CSR means that "they consider their social and environmental practices in tandem with considering their quality standards, financial stability, and fair pricing."[2] As early as 1984, Patagonia offered healthy, vegetarian food in its on-site cafeteria as well as on-site child care. Today, Patagonia engages in the following CSR practices: (a) audits to ensure good working conditions exist in factories; (b) preventing and eliminating

---

[1] Patagonia. (2021). *Patagonia Macro Puff Quilt*. https://www.patagonia.com/product/macro-puff-outdoor-quilt/22110.html?dwvar_22110_color=FGDB&cgid=luggage-sleeping-bagshttps://www.patagonia.com/product/macro-puff-outdoor-quilt/22110.html?dwvar_22110_color=FGDB&cgid=luggage-sleeping-bags.

[2] Patagonia. (2021). *A history of our environmental and social responsibility*. https://www.patagonia.com/our-footprint/corporate-social-responsibility-history.html.

sweatshops; (c) tracking the social and environmental impact of the products it sells; (d) ensuring that Asian migrants are not forced into labor and debt bondage; (e) considering living wages when assigning workplace policies and salaries; (f) initiating a Fair Trade Certified label, for which a percentage of the money from the sale of Patagonia items that have this label goes directly to the workers at the particular plant where these items were produced; (g) expanding this fair trade from India to other countries; (h) allowing migrant workers to have and use their voice; and (i) using sustainable fibers. Both in recognition of the fact that new Patagonia merchandise can be expensive and limit the consumer base as well as trying to reduce carbon footprint and waste (by 73%), Patagonia also allows individuals to trade in old Patagonia, get credit for new merchandise, and resell old items for a much reduced cost with a space for this on their website, Patagonia Worn Wear.[3] The sum of these responsible actions reveal that Patagonia is taking a moral stance. Against climate change. Against waste. And against mistreatment of people from marginalized backgrounds throughout the world. Part of their mission statement is "We seek not only to do less harm, but more good." Consistent with this, in 2022 founder Yvon Chouinard gave the company away by relinquishing ownership so that its profits would be used to combat climate change.[4]

This notion of "more good" is the basis of CSR—a moral obligation to do well. The concept of CSR dates back to the 17th and 18th centuries with Locke and Rousseau's notion of the social contract of mutual obligations. The idea is that organizations share responsibility for the social good of a community in which they operate. So organizations should operate their businesses ethically and be held accountable to themselves, their stakeholders, and the public. Organizations should not do anything that knowingly harms stakeholders, and if they do, they should rectify it.

---

[3] Patagonia. (2021). *Worn Wear*. https://wornwear.patagonia.com.
[4] Gelles, D. (2022, September 14). Billionaire no more: Patagonia founder gives away the company. *The New York Times*. https://www.nytimes.com/2022/09/14/climate/patagonia-climate-philanthropy-chouinard.html.

The concept of CSR, both in name and unnamed but in practice, has seen a resurgence of interest. Perhaps with the emergence of climate change, a global pandemic, political polarization, and widespread social movements, organizations have come to understand that they are compelled to take a moral standpoint. One critical area for such CSR is in diversity, equity, and inclusion (DEI) practices.

Indeed, there is a moral imperative for DEI. The MBA students in our class described this in a variety of ways. One student noted, "Providing everyone the same opportunities to succeed and be treated with respect equally is just the right thing to do." Another stated, "It is important to strive for a society in which everyone has the opportunity to improve their lives through meaningful work." Still another student summed it up by stating "diversity is the right thing to do."

The rationale underlying this idea of *doing the right thing* was also reflected by a member of the MBA class who immigrated to the United States:

> The effects of slavery are extremely mindboggling. Forcefully and deceitfully taking people away from their birth country, dehumanizing them and treating them worse than pigs for 250 years. Then setting them "free" (on paper) while enforcing systems of division and laws of segregation for another 100 years, while you amass land and property is just EVIL. This perfectly explains why African Americans are where they are today (struggling with low income jobs, lots of males locked up in jail, children growing up without father figures, communities without access to quality education, people with severe mental health issues etc.). So yes, there is a MORAL case for enforcing diversity now to allow people [to] catch up those 400 years of OPPRESSION. In my opinion, it is the most important reason.

This moral case for DEI centers around the notion that every employee should have an equal opportunity to gain access, develop, progress, and be productive at work. This perspective of DEI as an ethical issue appeals to a core human belief in fairness and justice. These social norms, or basic expectations about human interaction, shape the societies in which we live and work. The moral imperative—that DEI is the right, just, and fair thing to do—may in fact be the most effective argument toward social change.[5]

Tools for Working Together

1. The following quotes are ones that we have repeatedly heard articulated by thought leaders:
   - "Organizations need to do good work for their broader communities and societies" (corporate social responsibility).
   - "The moral imperative is actually necessary to create a truly inclusive organization because it means the organization is not just checking the box and trying to increase representation for a business argument/for a legal requirement."
   - "The organization cares about doing the right thing and will embrace the associated challenges, which employees and the broader public care about."
     a. Do any of these quotes resonate with you or what you hear from those in your organization?
     b. How do these quotes illustrate the moral imperative of diversity?
     c. What other, similar moral arguments have you heard that are compelling?
2. Why is it important for leaders to foster an inclusive organizational climate and choose to operate in ways that benefit the public good?
3. What beneficial outcomes arise when an organization encourages an inclusive organizational culture and implements socially responsible business practices?
4. What policies, practices, or norms could your organization put in place to better leverage the moral imperative of diversity?

---

[5] Sonenshein, S. (2006). Crafting social issues at work. *Academy of Management Journal, 49,* 1158–1172.

5. Reflect on all three imperatives of diversity discussed so far in this book, namely the realistic, business, and moral imperatives.
   a. Which imperative is most compelling to you personally?
   b. Which do you think is the strongest argument for optimizing diversity in the future workforce?
   c. What is a potential problem of relying on only one argument?

5
Are There Downsides to Diversity?

Demands due to both the COVID-19 pandemic and a general aging of the population will lead to an estimated 200,000–450,000 nursing shortage by 2025.[1] One of the many ways that U.S. hospitals are dealing with the short staffing is to hire more nurses from overseas.[2] Unfortunately, this increase in diversity may create what Galanti terms a "breeding ground for conflict and misunderstanding, which can result in tension among the staff and inferior patient care."[3] Galanti, a leading health expert in the field of cultural competencies, further describes a number of examples in which diversity may lead to problematic outcomes. One example involves a difference between collectivist countries (e.g., those in Asia) and individualistic countries (e.g., those in North America), which often reveals that Asian workers generally want to avoid conflict, show respect for authority, and avoid disagreement. However, there are cases in the medical field in which it is important to disagree and be assertive (e.g., checking the right medicine dosages and operating with the correct tools on the correct body part); thus, diversity may lead to negative outcomes. Another example involves the intersection between country of origin and gender. In some cases, men from certain countries (e.g., Nigeria and countries in the Middle East) may have difficulty taking orders from women. Thus, a Nigerian registered

---

[1] McKinsey & Company. (2022, May 11). *Assessing the lingering impact of COVID-19 on the nursing workforce.* https://www.mckinsey.com/industries/healthcare-systems-and-services/our-insights/assessing-the-lingering-impact-of-covid-19-on-the-nursing-workforce.

[2] Ehli, N. (2022, January 6). Short-staffed and COVID-battered, U.S. hospitals are hiring more foreign nurses. *Shots: Heath News from NPR.* https://www.npr.org/sections/health-shots/2022/01/06/1069369625/short-staffed-and-covid-battered-u-s-hospitals-are-hiring-more-foreign-nurses.

[3] Galanti, G. A. (2001). The challenge of serving and working with diverse populations in American hospitals. *Diversity Factor, 9*(3), 21–26. https://hsc.unm.edu/community/toolkit/docs8/culturaldiversity.pdf.

nurse may have trouble following direct orders from an American female doctor. Galanti generally talks about the importance of education and training, and we wholeheartedly agree, but why do these downsides occur?

One of the most well-known adages that is taught in introductory social psychology classes throughout the United States is that "birds of a feather flock together." Indeed, one of the greatest predictors of who likes each other across a widespread set of contexts for an extended period of time is similarity.[4] How similar are you to another person? Similarity in "attractiveness," attitudes, and political views. The more similar, the more likely you are to become acquainted, become friends, and remain together. Research by Chris Crandall and colleagues[5] suggests that the extent to which you get along with another person may well be predicted before you even meet that person.

The reason for this is that it is more difficult to interact with people who are different. Differing views can cause conflict. Conflict challenges people to work harder, to have to listen to opinions that are far different from one's own.[6] It causes people to be less sure of themselves and to have interactions that may be less comfortable. Yet, differing views can also be very helpful—they provide new ideas, provide you with safeguards to making bad decisions, and help you expand your knowledge base. To that point, two Supreme Court justices, Ruth Bader Ginsburg and Antonin Scalia, were on ideological sides that vastly opposed each other. It is difficult to imagine that their families would get along so well, particularly in today's climate, where politics are tearing families and friendships apart. But indeed, it seems that in addition to starkly disagreeing with each other politically throughout their careers, they both had many things in common: They were both from New York, they were approximately

---

[4] Byrne, D. (1997). An overview (and underview) of research and theory within the attraction paradigm. *Journal of Social and Personal Relationships, 14,* 417–431.

[5] Bahns, A. J., Crandall, C. S., Gillath, O., & Preacher, K. J. (2017). Similarity in relationships as niche construction: Choice, stability, and influence within dyads in a free choice environment. *Journal of Personality and Social Psychology, 112*(2), 329–355.

[6] Moran, B. (2018, July 30). Diversity is difficult. *The Brink: Pioneering Research from Boston University.* https://www.bu.edu/articles/2018/diversity-is-difficult.

the same age, they shared a love of opera, they sometimes traveled together, and their families spent many New Year's Eves together.

Are there downsides to diversity? The short answer is yes, there can be. A balanced conversation about diversity in organizations does not just include talking about the benefits; it also includes talking about the challenges. And there can certainly be challenges to having diversity within groups of people and organizations. We discuss six potential downsides that are commonly mentioned in the literature and in the experiences of our MBA students' working careers.

First, diversity often removes people from their comfort zones. As one of our MBA students noted, "A downside of diversity is that it can lead to discomfort." People tend to prefer a homeostasis where they feel comfortable and can predict situations. Being around people who share similarities can provide a comforting sense of predicting and knowing how others will think, perceive, and act. This sense of comfort does not always happen when there is diversity among co-workers. Similarly, people may feel threatened by diversity initiatives, which remind them of a changing demography and move away toward what is the current status quo. Diversity initiatives may erroneously be interpreted as valuing one set of people over another, and this ideology results in less, rather than more, support. A number of studies have shown that some individuals (particularly White men) react negatively toward increasing diversity because they view it as a zero-sum game in which more of "them" means less of "us." A member of our MBA class reflected this perspective when stating, "I believe it has been harder for me to get hired and move up within a company because of my race (White), gender (man), and age (older)." Diversity is often incorrectly perceived as a free handout for minority groups, which leads to animosity toward members of underrepresented groups that are doing well and receiving opportunities.

Second, diversity can lead to mistrust, miscommunication, and conflict issues. At times, people ignore information that does not coincide with their own beliefs, especially when it comes from somebody they do not like or do not trust. Diversity can essentially lessen the initial trust that others have with each other and lead people to clash over opposing viewpoints. Also, it is sometimes difficult to get people from diverse backgrounds on the same page, particularly when they define problems differently and believe in different solutions. As one of our MBA students stated,

> Although the advantages outweigh the disadvantages, there are some cons of diversity in the workplace. . . . I work in teams of 20 people representing 12 nationalities across 4 continents. Sometimes, there are too many opinions . . . which in turn creates dissension over time. Some members stop sharing ideas in consequent meetings.

Third, diversity initiatives may lead people to believe that they are being told how to think and act, which can give rise to a range of unfavorable reactions. For instance, one MBA student said, "Sometimes diversity leads people to become afraid of speaking their truth." People might respond with a sense of resistance. Resistance may cause some people to consciously and actively work against diversity, equity, and inclusion (DEI)—such initiatives can indeed meet backlash. It is also possible that people respond unconsciously to increasing heterogeneity with homophily, a tendency to associate with similar others that is not so different from segregation. Independently and in conjunction with each other, these conscious and unconscious reactions can lead to increases in biases, not decreases.

Fourth, targets may also react negatively or suffer, even when the diversity initiatives are often intended to help them. If diversity is tied to achieving a certain number or percentage of people, it can make others view diversity negatively and lead others to view people from marginalized backgrounds as rivals. This is not to say that targets are not helpful; in fact, many of these aspirational goals lead to actual increases in otherwise underrepresentation (e.g., Enbridge states that it is targeting 40% representation of women by 2025)[7],

---

[7] Enbridge. (2022, March, 8). *Celebrating accomplishments, committing to change on International Women's Day*. https://www.enbridge.com/stories/2022/march/international-womens-day-celebrating-accomplishments-committing-to-change.

but diversity initiatives also have the potential to make targets feel ostracized and "less-than" than other employees. This was a common theme that our MBA students reported. For instance, one of our Black MBA students wrote,

> My achievements and hard work are undermined as just being part of the diversity initiative. It even makes me question myself sometimes "Did they just hire me because I am black?" I do not want to be hired or rejected because of the color of my skin. I just want to be treated fairly.

A female MBA student wrote,

> As a woman who constantly enters work groups that are only men, I can feel the air being sucked out of the room when I come in . . . that can be incredibly isolating. Even though diversity is good and moral in the workplace, facing resistance is challenging and emotionally taxing.

Similarly, another student wrote that "Affirmative action makes it so people feel like I (a minority) have not earned my achievements/scholarship. People have made comments like 'you only got your scholarship because you're Mexican.'" These kinds of perceptions and attributions can severely undermine the experiences of people from marginalized backgrounds.

Fifth, diversity is often left in the hands of one unprepared individual or of workers in human resources (HR) functions. And if that individual is not respected, or if the HR division as a whole is not a respected entity within an organization, it can be really problematic and difficult to make changes. As one MBA student said, "I do believe there can be downsides when it comes to the people in the workplace who initiate and maintain [diversity initiatives]. Some people are not as open-minded as others and may make implementations of D&I initiatives more difficult." Similarly, another MBA student wrote "One problem is that leaders often lack the ability to manage diversity and engage in inclusive leadership." We agree that the effectiveness of DEI strategies and programs likely depends on both the actual and the perceived knowledge, skills, and abilities of the people who are involved.

Sixth, creating and sustaining DEI is hard work. There is no single silver bullet, no magic wand that can create immediate and long-lasting organizational change. The resources that are necessary to move toward DEI—such as time, energy, and financial commitments—can be substantial.

Although we have discussed six of the challenges to diversity, there are many more. The MBA students in our class mentioned other downsides, including the following:

- Those who most need to hear DEI messages can often avoid diversity training because it is often optional.
- People who do not have to have DEI conversations often feel little or no empathy toward the push for greater DEI.
- People often try to get a certain number of diverse candidates to apply for jobs just so they can check off a number.
- Diversity can negatively affect productivity due to the shift of people's differences without systems of support.
- Organizational infrastructure and support often do not accompany the presence of diversity into organizations.

Although there are challenges and downsides to diversity, these are far outweighed by the realistic, financial, and moral imperatives of DEI. Moreover, understanding some of the issues that stand in the way of DEI can help minimize its risks and maximize its benefits. In Section 2, we focus on challenges that get in the way of working together with these goals in mind.

Tools for Working Together

1. Have you ever had problems working with co-workers who are different from you? How were they different? What sort of problems arose from these differences?

2. What other downsides to diversity have you experienced or witnessed in your organization?
3. Can you think of any way in which the downsides might have been avoided? Are there strategies that you think the organization might have adopted to eliminate the problems associated with differences?

SECTION 2

BIASES THAT HOLD US BACK FROM WORKING TOGETHER

Imagine being a female worker at an automobile plant surrounded by male coworkers. On your first tour of the plant, your new male colleagues catcall, whistle, scream, and howl at you. Later, they call you offensive names and tell you that you are not welcome at the plant. In training, the men in the company state that they do not believe women should work in the factories. Over the course of your first few years there, they add sexual graffiti to cars coming down the assembly line and post pictures, names, and phone numbers of you and your female colleagues in the men's bathrooms. As time goes by, they begin to tell you obscene jokes, simulate masturbation, and actually fondle and expose themselves in front of you. These same male colleagues are paying young women to have sex in a back room of the plant, and the company is hosting sex parties and company events that include dinners, drinks, strippers, and prostitutes. Some of your female colleagues quit, but you decide to stay and try to get promoted. Your manager tells you that your promotion is premised on your willingness to grant sexual favors.

All of these details really happened.[1] Yes, this unsavory set of details is a reality for the women who worked at Mitsubishi in the Normal, Illinois, plant during the years of 1988–1993.[2] The company was charged with allowing a hostile setting for women and settled

---

[1] Braun, S. (1998, June 12). Mitsubishi to pay $34 million in sex harassment case. *Los Angeles Times*. https://www.latimes.com/archives/la-xpm-1998-jun-12-mn-59249-story.html.
[2] *EEOC v. Mitsubishi Motor Manufacturing of America*, No. 96-1192.

for $34 million, and it also paid additional millions in individual lawsuits.

You might think this type of outdated example of discrimination against women no longer exists. And yet, in June 2022, a class-action lawsuit against Sterling Jewelers (a conglomerate that includes Kay Jewelers, Zales, and Jared the Galleria of Jewelry) resulted in a $125 million dollar payout to approximately 68,000 former and current female employees based on unfair pay and promotion they experienced. Many of these women also provided testimony revealing that they had been harassed, groped, and pressured into providing sexual favors.[3] Further details suggest that female employees complained that managers had scouting parties to identify female employees they wanted to have sex with, they made fun of and nicknamed women based on their body parts, women were passed over for promotions, and women were told that other women did not get promotions because of their looks.[4,5] In another example, in November 2021, racist and misogynist comments were left anonymously on a shared document for medical students who pool information and tips each year about upcoming medical "matches."[6]

Why do these events happen? What might lead people to engage in such offensive behavior? In this section of the book, we discuss the psychological processes—stereotypes and prejudice—that give rise to and sustain individual behaviors and organizational structures that are discriminatory. We distinguish the overt harassment

---

[3] Harwell, D. (2022, June 9). Jewelry giant settles gender-discrimination lawsuit for $175 million. *The Washington Post.* https://www.washingtonpost.com/business/2022/06/09/sterling-kay-jared-sex-dscrimination.

[4] Harwell, D. (2017, February 28). Widespread sex harassment alleged at jewelry giant. *The Washington Post.* https://www.washingtonpost.com/business/economy/kay-and-jared-jewerly-giant-calls-sex-harassment-claims-a-purported-parallel-universe/2017/03/09/3c93a93a-04dc-11e7-ad5b-d22680e18d10_story.html.

[5] Brodresser-Akner, T. (2019, April 23). The company that sells love to America had a dark secret. *The New York Times.* https://www.nytimes.com/2019/04/23/magazine/kay-jewelry-sexual-harassment.html?.

[6] McFarling, U. L. (2021, December 13). The whitest specialty: As medicine strives to close its diversity gaps, one field remains a stubborn outlier. STAT. https://www.statnews.com/2021/12/13/whitest-specialty-as-medicine-strives-to-close-diversity-gaps-orthopedic-surgery-remains-stubborn-outlier.

described above from more subtle forms of bias that contribute to inequities, hostile environments, and problematic workplaces. We review the psychological explanations for bias and describe how discrimination is manifested by individuals and organizations; understanding why and how bias exists is a critical step toward its remediation.

6
Psychological Explanations for Bias

Brave research assistants in our lab sometimes serve as actors in our experiments. In one set of studies, these undergraduates were asked to wear obesity prostheses, or in other words, "fat suits." These costumes were professionally constructed by a designer who stuffed soft cotton ball–like material between inner and outer layers of clothes. The inner layers of the pants and shirt were chosen to fit women who were thin, and the outer layers made them appear to be much larger in size. In a matter of seconds, the size 4–8 actors were transformed to a size 22. Our data consistently showed that people were treated more negatively when they wore the fat suit (appear to be obese) than when they did not. Although our researchers acted happy to put on the prostheses and perform the studies, they were far more relieved to be able to take them off at the end of the day. In the street, in the mall, and on job interviews, these research assistants/actors received less eye contact and friendly treatment, and more hostility and rudeness, when they were wearing the fat suit. People stood farther away from them and spent less time talking to them when they were wearing the fat suit. In other words, people discriminated against those whom they believed to be obese.

Obesity is a condition that is perceived extremely negatively in contemporary American society; many Americans believe that obese people are lazy and undisciplined, and even disgusting.[1] A study of top executives showed that even chief executive officers (CEOs) who are obese are rated as less effective leaders by their peers and subordinates compared to CEOs who are thin.[2] It is clear that these negative beliefs are also associated with negative attitudes

---

[1] Crandall, C. S., Merman, A., & Hebl, M. (2009). Anti-fat prejudice. In T. D. Nelson (Ed.), *Handbook of prejudice, stereotyping, and discrimination* (pp. 469–487). Psychology Press.
[2] King, E. B., Rogelberg, S. G., Hebl, M. R., Braddy, P. W., Shanock, L. R., Doerer, S. C., & McDowell-Larsen, S. (2016). Waistlines and ratings of executives: Does executive status

about people who are obese—just listen to a few "fat jokes" on YouTube.

But why? Why would someone's body size have anything to do with others' reactions to them? Why do biases exist? This chapter begins with a series of examples that demonstrate some of the fundamental processes that sustain biases, preserve the status quo, and often keep organizations from creating diversity, equity, and inclusion (DEI) initiatives.

Mental Shortcuts Can Get in the Way

Psychologists have identified dozens of systematic human biases. When we hear new information (whether it is an initial medical diagnosis or a first offer for buying a car), we have an anchoring bias—that first piece of information has a greater effect on our decision-making than any other information. Humans have a hindsight bias that makes us think we could have predicted events that are random (e.g., a coin toss).

To demonstrate how cognitive processes can interfere with information processing, let's consider a few examples. First, compare the color of the squares to which the lines with arrows A and B are pointing in Figure 6.1.

Do you think these squares are the same colors, or are they different colors? What do you think? Are they the same, or are they different? If you said that they are different, you are not alone. But what if we told you they are the same color, and you are just seeing things in a biased way. Would you believe that? Would you believe that you are biased?

Indeed, this illusion is called Adelson's checker-shadow illusion.[3] The fact is that the two squares are the same color. Next, you will see

---

overcome obesity stigma? *Human Resource Management*, 55(2), 283–300. https://doi.org/10.1002/hrm.21267.

[3] Thomson, G., & Macpherson, F. (2017, July). Adelson's checker-shadow illusion. In F. Macpherson (Ed.), *The illusions index*. https://www.illusionsindex.org/ir/20-checkershadow..

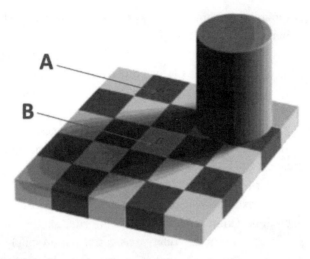

Figure 6.1 Checker-shadow illusion.
Source: Copyright Edward Adelson.

Figure 6.2 Checker-shadow illusion, cropped.
Source: Copyright Edward Adelson.

how we prove this—we just cut off the sides (Figure 6.2). As you can see, the two squares are identical in color. The original surroundings of the two just make them appear different.

This image, the checker-shadow illusion, forms part of an optical illusion activity that was published by Edward H. Adelson, Professor of Vision Science at Massachusetts Institute of Technology, in 1995 (Adelson, 2005). It demonstrates how human unconscious beliefs can distort human perception. In Figure 6.2, by joining squares A and B with two vertical stripes of the same shade of gray, it becomes apparent that both squares are the same color. The human brain might not believe what it is seeing because no matter how long one looks at the first image, the brain will see two squares of different colors. This optical illusion places emphasis on the significance of relativity when attempting to measure things or perceiving people, places, and things—and the effects of perspective, in this case light and shadow (Adelson, 2005). What people see changes according to how they see it. Thus, both perspective and reality determine values and behavior.

Similarly, the human brain unconsciously filters and categorizes incoming information, so humans perceive reality according to their own expectations. Humans tend to accept information that confirms their beliefs (which scholars refer to as confirmation bias) and ignore information that challenges those beliefs, rather interpreting information in ways that support prior beliefs (which scholars refer to as myside bias) (Mercier & Sperber, 2017).

Adelson's checkerboard illusion helps us better understand biases and reflect on what this illusion reveals about the human brain's ability to perceive objective reality. We think we see the world as it is, but that is not always true. In the case of the squares, our brains are using relative information—the shades of boxes A and B in relation to the boxes closest to them—rather than making an absolute judgment. Our brains are taking shortcuts. This sometimes serves us well by allowing us to make quicker decisions and to save some of our cognitive resources (our brainpower) for other needs. Yet, as in the case of the shades of A and B, these shortcuts can also get in the way of us interpreting information accurately. The term *heuristics* refers to the automatic, often subconscious, decision-making processes in the human brain. As Noble laureate Danny Kahneman reminds us,[4] these processes allow for faster, more energy-efficient decisions that generally help us deal effectively with the world around us.

Now consider another example. When you look at Figure 6.3, do the horizontal lines look like they are at an angle, or do they appear to be exactly parallel to each other? Does the picture appear as a

---

[4] Kahneman, D. (2011). *Thinking, fast and slow*. Macmillan.

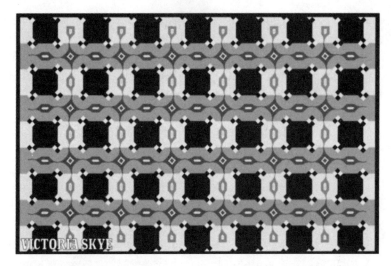

Figure 6.3 Café wall optical illusion.

ramp with four different slants, or does it appear to have four horizontal lines that are equally parallel?

Figure 6.3 is a version of the café wall optical illusion[5] or an updated version of Münsterberg's illusion.[6] Most individuals see these lines as slanted. But if you look again (or narrow your line of vision), you will see that they are perfectly parallel. It is the alternating pattern of vertical lines that tricks your brain.

Different types of biases trick us into thinking we are objective interpreters of reality, when in fact, all humans process information inaccurately. Our brains are wired to try to reduce their workload and preserve cognitive resources. We often use all kinds of shortcuts to try to understand the world around us as quickly and easily as possible.

Think for a moment about the chair that you sat in the last time you went out for dinner. Most of you probably can't remember that (or even the place you went to dinner). If you can remember, the

---

[5] Skye, V. (2017). *Skye Blue café wall illusion.* http://www.victoriaskye.com.
[6] Münsterberg, H. (1897). Die verschobene Schachbrettfigur. *Zeitschrift für Psychologie, 15,* 184–188.

chair was probably some object that had a flat surface, perpendicular to another flat surface, with three or four parallel columns holding it up. Before you went to sit in that chair, did you stop to worry that it would collapse when you did sit? Did you think about the object at all? You probably didn't. You saw the object and your brain processed the relevant geometric characteristics in less than a second.

In the case of the chair, your brain's shortcuts helped you sit comfortably with minimal cognitive effort or resources. In the case of the biases and illusions demonstrated in Figure 6.3, however, your brain's shortcuts got in the way of you interpreting information and making decisions accurately. The same kinds of problems can emerge when biases interfere with interpersonal interactions.

What is crucial for DEI is acknowledging that we hold biases about not only checkerboards and lines but also *people*. These are sometimes referred to as unconscious biases or subtle biases. (Rather than distinguishing whether these biases are unconscious, conscious, or semiconscious, we refer to them as "subtle" biases.) These biases are what some people refer to as equal opportunity viruses. Each of us can get infected, even if we think that we are protected.

Take a moment to think about your co-workers. Think about the last three or four colleagues with whom you have most recently interacted. How biased are these co-workers of you? How much do they engage in stereotyping? How prejudiced are they? Or just, as a whole, how biased are they? Choose a number on the following scale:

1.......2.......3.......4.......5.......6.......7

Not at all biased   Somewhat biased   Extremely biased

Have you selected your number? Don't change that number, and try to remember it for later.

Now, we want you to focus on you. How biased are you? How often do you stereotype others? How prejudiced are you? Overall, how biased are *you*? Again, choose a number on the scale, somewhere between 1 and 7. Do you have that number? Don't read on until you have that number selected.

Now, compare the two sets of numbers. Who did you indicate was more biased, your co-workers or you? If your answer is your co-workers, then you are like most people. We acknowledge that if you are reading this book, you are probably actively thinking about how to engage with DEI initiatives, so it may well be that they are less biased. However, most people think that *others* are much more biased than they are.

This is just one of a number of self-serving biases we have. We tend to believe that we are better than others and are just more immune to cognitive errors than other people. We believe that we have the ability to be impartial and make very objective evaluations. But, of course, we can't all be better than average. Not surprisingly, these biases extend to a variety of domains—most of us think that compared to other people, we are better drivers, we are smarter, we are more creative, and we are even more attractive than most other people. These self-serving biases, together with biases that are based on social group memberships, are the building blocks of stereotypes and prejudice.

Stereotypes

Stereotypes are widely held but fixed and oversimplified images or ideas about particular types of persons and things. Stereotypes can be really helpful. They are cognitive shortcuts that we rely on to make determinations about people. We might use these stereotypes to make predictions.

Vehicle Stereotypes

We can predict who drives what kinds of vehicles. Who do you think drives the vehicle in Figure 6.4A? If you answered a soccer mom or certainly someone who has a family, you wouldn't be alone. Similarly, who drives the vehicle pictured in Figure 6.4B? Maybe a masculine guy, someone who hunts or fishes, or someone who works in construction? Are these stereotypes accurate? Sometimes, but certainly not all the time. We all have these stereotypes, and we all use them.

Figure 6.4 Vehicle stereotypes.
Sources: A, nitinut380/Shutterstock; B, Roman Belogorodov/Shutterstock.

Figure 6.5 CEO stereotypes.

We can't get rid of them because they are based on cultural information and knowledge. So just living in our society, we learn cultural information, we learn stereotypes.

We also have stereotypes about certain types of people. When we think about CEOs and schoolteachers, we have gender stereotypes. If we told you some of the people pictured in Figure 6.5 were CEOs and some were schoolteachers, who would you put into which category? The problem is that stereotypes are sometimes wrong, and they are misleading. In this case, if you said that the two women were the CEOs, you would be correct. They are the CEOs of Synchrony (Margaret Keane) and Levi's (Michelle Gass). The two men, however, are award-winning schoolteachers—Greg Oubre, elementary school teacher of the year from Waco, Texas, and George Padilla, high school teacher of the year from Bel Air High School in Texas.

Another way to understand the limiting and often negative gender stereotypes that exist in the workplace is to consider the stereotype

Table 6.1 Labels for Stern Male and Female Leaders

	Stern Female Leaders	Stern Male Leaders
Female protégé	A "The queen bee"	B No known label
Male protégé	C No known label	D No known label

of women working together. The content of such stereotypes often reveals that female co-workers do not seem to be able to get along with each other and/or female leaders particularly treat their female subordinates harshly. This latter scenario has been so sensationalized that these women are given a name and referred to as "queen bees," if not a more profane word choice. However, data do not pan out in showing that women tend to be particularly negative toward other women.[7,8] One way that we can explain the strong, resistant beliefs that people have about the queen bee phenomenon is to consider the fact that people pay attention to behaviors that confirm their beliefs more than behaviors that disconfirm their beliefs.[9] Table 6.1 depicts "stern" female or male leaders leading male or female protégés. If people believe in the queen bee or have access to this stereotype, then they overfocus on all the instances that fall into cell A, and they ignore or downplay all of the instances that occur in the other cells. In addition, what label do we give to the other cells? None come to mind as quickly as does the queen bee, again solidifying its status as an overprescribed myth that is too often accepted. The next time you think about a woman treating another woman badly, ask yourself, Are you overfocusing on cell A?

Now, all of us, even the most well-intentioned, are subject to these biases. One exercise you can do that can raise your awareness of the

---

[7] Arvate, P. R., Galilea, G. W., & Todescat, I. (2018). The queen bee: A myth? The effect of top-level female leadership on subordinate females. *The Leadership Quarterly, 29*(5), 533–548.
[8] Sheppard, L. D., & Aquino, K. (2013). Much ado about nothing? Observers' problematization of women's same-sex conflict at work. *Academy of Management Perspectives, 27*(1), 52–62.
[9] Gilovich, T. (1993). *How we know what isn't so: The fallibility of human reason in everyday life.* Free Press.

kinds of stereotypes that might affect you is the Implicit Association Test.[10] This is a popular tool that shows the strength of associations we have between certain aspects of identity (e.g., gender, race, and obesity) and certain stereotypes. The test is a bit controversial among researchers in terms of measurement, but it is a widely available option for beginning to understand your own stereotypes. Some stereotypes affect the workplace more than do others. Age-related stereotypes particularly can have dramatic effects on who gets hired, evaluated favorably, promoted, and let go. An article published online by the Society of Human Resource Management (SHRM)[11] discussed the five age stereotypes that workplaces need to eradicate: Older workers cost too much, are afraid of technology, are not motivated, get sick more often, and are resistant to change. There are also stereotypes that older workers are more difficult to train, poor performers, and less productive.

Just as there are stereotypes about older workers, there are also stereotypes about younger workers. It is a fairly common experience for us (and maybe for you) to hear someone talk pejoratively about "those millennials." Best described as those born between 1981 and 1996, millennials are commonly stereotyped as being poorly prepared for the workforce, lazy, lacking ambition, focused more on their personal lives, entitled, job-hoppers, and don't have time for older workers telling them what to do. Eden reported on research[12] examining more than 20,000 employees across 20 different studies who spanned multigenerational groups, and the sweeping differences in preferences and values depending on age or generation alone were not supported. In fact, an examination of America's past indicates that many of the stereotypes that exist today about

---

[10] If you visit Project Implicit or https://implicit.harvard.edu/implicit/aboutus.html, you can take a brief test and get a sense of the degree to which you are quicker to associate some identities with particular ideas than others (e.g., men and teaching vs. women and teaching).
[11] Nagele-Piazza, L. (2017, November). *5 age stereotypes workplaces need to eradicate.* SHRM. https://www.shrm.org/resourcesandtools/legal-and-compliance/employment-law/pages/5-age-stereotypes-workplaces-need-to-eradicate.aspx.
[12] King, E., Finkelstein, L., Thomas, C., & Corrington, A. (2019, August). Generational differences at work are small: Thinking they're big affects our behavior. *Harvard Business Review.*

young workers are the same ones that existed decades ago. So if you find yourself beginning to think regularly and often that "today's kids are lazy" and "they just don't wanna work," you might just be aging yourself!

Research from prominent psychologists[13] suggests that, in general, beliefs about people from different social groups can be understood along two primary dimensions. Specifically, stereotypes vary with regard to perceptions of (a) competence and (b) warmth. This means that we tend to view people from some groups as more competent (confident, assertive, and capable) than people from other groups and that we think people from some groups are warmer (sincere, kind, and generous) than people from other groups. Men tend to be stereotyped as higher in competence but lower in warmth than women. People who are obese are stereotyped as low in both competence and warmth.

This stereotype content model is helpful in understanding the dominant cognitive structures or belief systems that feed into bias against people from a variety of social groups. What is important about all of these stereotypes is that they can begin to take on a life of their own. That is, when people hold these stereotypes, they may be more likely to engage in prejudice and discrimination, which we discuss in more detail next.

Prejudice

Prejudice involves attitudes or feelings toward people because they belong to a certain group. If stereotypes suggest that men are more competent and women are warmer, gendered prejudice might include attitudes that men should be the breadwinners and women should be the homemakers. Consistent with this, one form of

---

[13] Fiske, S. T., Cuddy, A. J., Glick, P., & Xu, J. (2002). A model of (often mixed) stereotype content: Competence and warmth respectively follow from perceived status and competition. *Journal of Personality and Social Psychology, 82*(6), 878–902.

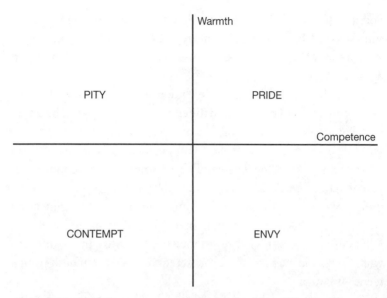

Figure 6.6 Perceptions of warmth and competence.

prejudice against women is the attitude that they should be responsible for cooking, cleaning, and taking care of children.

More generally, the stereotype content model suggests that stereotypes drive emotional responses.[14] The extent to which we perceive people from a particular group to be warm and competent will influence the favorability of our response. Figure 6.6 depicts how varying aspects of warmth and competence in targets are perceived by others. Evidence from throughout the world suggests that prejudice toward people who are perceived to be both warm and competent tends to be favorable; people who are warm and competent are admired and garner pride. Attitudes about people from groups that are viewed as lacking in both warmth and competence are instead imbued with contempt. Mixed reactions emerge for people from groups that are high in perceptions of either warmth or

---

[14] Fiske, S. T., Cuddy, A. J., Glick, P., & Xu, J. (2002). A model of (often mixed) stereotype content: Competence and warmth respectively follow from perceived status and competition. *Journal of Personality and Social Psychology, 82*(6), 878–902.

competence but not both. People from groups that are stereotyped as high in warmth but low in competence evoke pity, whereas people from groups that are stereotyped as high in competence but low in warmth tend to evoke envy.

Taken together, this means that prejudice toward groups such as Christians (high warmth, high competence) tends to evoke admiration, prejudice toward the rich (low warmth, high competence) tends to give rise to envy, prejudice toward people with disabilities (high warmth, low competence) involves pity, and prejudice toward people who are without homes (low warmth, low competence) looks like outright contempt. As you might imagine, people behave very differently toward others depending on whether they feel contempt versus admiration or pity.

Stereotypes and prejudices are thus ambivalent—both positive and negative—and can change over time. Indeed, as an example, a complex set of beliefs and attitudes has emerged in reference to Asian Americans. Often referred to as the model minority, Asian American people are frequently held up as stereotypical exemplars of how "good minorities" should be and act—smart, particularly good at STEM (science, technology, engineering, and mathematics), hardworking, docile, wealthy, and thin. Yet, at the same time, Asian American people are perceived as cold, sly, exotic, "foreign," and often only allied with White people when it serves White people. This often simultaneously wedges disharmony against other minority groups. In terms of the stereotype content model, Asian American people have been stereotyped as being high in competence but low in warmth. Confusion and blame over the origin of the COVID-19 pandemic have affected these stereotypes, and new forms of prejudice have been unleashed toward Asian American people. These emerging biases have yielded terrible incidents of discrimination, the topic of focus in Chapter 7.

Whereas prejudice involves attitudes, discrimination involves behaviors. Imagine seeing the name Mohammed Akhtar on a resume that is submitted for a teaching position. Stereotypes might make us think that the applicant is Muslim, Middle Eastern, and terrorist. The prejudices that accompany our stereotypes might make us feel like he would not be a trusted employee; we might think he is lacking warmth, so we might not like him. Discrimination toward job applicants can result directly from the stereotypes and prejudice associated with a particular name. Research on real job applications found that given the exact same resume, applicants named Emily and Greg (presumably White names) were more likely to be hired than applicants named Lakisha or Jamal (ostensibly Black names).[15] The act of giving a job or an interview to one candidate over another because of the identity indicated by their name is an act of discrimination. We consider both overt and more subtle forms of discrimination as meaningful aspects of bias.

Tools for Working Together

1. Please watch the TedX talk titled "The Danger of a Single Story" by Chimamanda Ngozi Adichie.[16] In this video, Adichie reflects on her experience as a Nigerian woman who immigrated to the United States as a young adult. She encountered Western societal narratives that painted her culture and background as unidimensional—she was stereotyped as "African" and many people did not care to understand her multitude of unique experiences. She discusses how easy it can be to fall into the trap in which you group others based on commonly held misconceptions rooted in stereotypes.

   After you have engaged with the video, reflect on how you experience the dangers of a single story in your own life. Specifically, consider your overall reflections in response to the following questions:
   a. What single story do you think people may have of you?
   b. Which strategies have you used to reduce that single narrative?

---

[15] Bertrand, M., & Mullainathan, S. (2004). Are Emily and Greg more employable than Lakisha and Jamal? A field experiment on labor market discrimination. *American Economic Review, 94*(4), 991–1013.

[16] https://www.youtube.com/watch?v=D9Ihs241zeg&ab_channel=TED.

c. Do you think it is challenging to employ these strategies to reduce that single narrative?
   d. How do you think others could support you in your efforts?
2. There are many websites[17,18,19] that offer further information about the biases you and your colleagues in organizations may hold. We recommend visiting some of these websites to learn more about erroneous ways of thinking. Choose one or two of these biases and think about the way in which you may have seen them play out in your own organization.
   a. In what way was bias portrayed?
   b. What was the consequence of that bias?
   c. Would knowing about the bias potentially prevented any ramifications?

---

[17] https://thedecisionlab.com/biases.
[18] https://www.mentalfloss.com/article/68705/20-cognitive-biases-affect-your-decisions.
[19] https://storage.googleapis.com/titlemax-media/099372db-50-cognitive-biases-2_80 per.png.

7
Individual-Level Discrimination

In contrast to the explicit and overt form of harassment at the Mitsubishi plant described in the Section 2 introduction, the terms "hepeating," "manterrupting," and "mansplaining" refer to anecdotal reports of somewhat subtle forms of sexism. Hepeating is demonstrated when men appropriate women's ideas or contributions that were previously ignored. Manterrupting reflects men's tendency to interrupt women when they are speaking. Finally, mansplaining occurs when men explain something to women in a manner that (often mistakenly) assumes the women have no knowledge of the topic. These popularized terms provide descriptive labels for women's everyday experiences of subtle sexism at work. So common are these experiences, in fact, that Kim Goodwin (author of *Designing for the Digital Age*) made a chart (adapted in Figure 7.1) to convey the point.[1]

Both subtle and overt types of bias are important to understand, identify, and address in order to understand how discrimination is manifested by individuals in organizations. To that end, we describe each in this chapter.

Overt Discrimination

Overt discrimination is obvious discrimination on the basis of identities such as race, color, national origin, sex, religion, age, disability, veteran status, and/or physical or mental disability in any aspect of the employment cycle. It can typically be identified, observed, and quantified to some extent. It is harmful because it prevents

---

[1] Goodwin, K. (2009). *Designing for the digital age: How to create human-centered products and services*. Wiley.

Am I mansplaining?

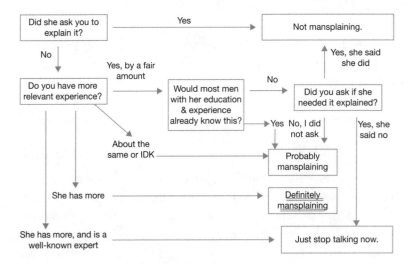

Figure 7.1 Am I mansplaining? IDK, I don't know.
Adapted from Goodwin, K. (2009). *Designing for the digital age: How to create human-centered products and services*. Wiley.

workplaces from being fair. It maintains the status quo by preventing certain people from advancing. It is costly to organizations. Most of all, it restricts talent.

A total of 38 of the 50 MBA students in our class reported that they had experienced overt types of discrimination. For instance, a female student in the entertainment business wrote, "Overt bias was part of the job description." She indicated that "it was extremely difficult to maintain good self-esteem when being told you are too big, too small, too tall, too blonde, not blonde enough, etc."

An Asian student stated,

> When I was working in a company, my boss instructed the ideal candidate for a new position. He said we are looking for a White, well connected, and educated professional. It was shocking for me that race and social status were defined from the beginning. When I went to talk with my boss, he told me that according to his experience, White, well-connected professionals are the ones that have better results.

A Black male MBA student stated that he had experienced "a lot" of overt discrimination. He indicated,

> From being overlooked for promotions to being given shitty projects . . . the field I work in can be particularly brutal. One example that sticks out was when a very top manager (a white man) who was a client had called me aside to tell me (I was the only black person in a work group of about 22), why he was justified to call another black person at his previous job site the n-word.

These examples are not just cherry-picked but are a real sampling of the examples of overt discrimination experienced by many of the MBA students. This form of discrimination is prohibited by a number of laws, such as Title VII of the Civil Rights Act, the Equal Pay Act, the Age Discrimination and Employment Act, the Rehabilitation Act, the Pregnancy Discrimination Act, and the Civil Rights Act of 1991. And there are various other laws that are based on municipal, city, and state legislation.

There are several categories of illegal, overt discrimination that should be understood. First is disparate treatment. This is intentional discrimination that happens when someone from a protected class is denied fair treatment in the workplace. So, for instance, let's say that to be promoted, women have to meet a certain standard that is much higher than that which men have to meet. They may have to generate a certain amount of sales, or they may have to have a certain amount of experience before they can make partner in a company. This kind of discrimination is overt, and it is based on being treated differently because of who a person is rather than the work that they do.

Another type of discrimination is adverse impact. Adverse impact can occur when an organization's policies or actions result in members of protected groups being negatively impacted. For instance, let's say there is a height requirement for a certain class of jobs that women cannot meet and, importantly, this height restriction is not necessary to do the job. Or let's say there are interview questions that inadvertently weed out more Black than White individuals, and the questions are not related to job performance. These examples reflect adverse impact if they meet the four-fifths rule, a selection rate for which one group of individuals is selected at less than 80% of another group of individuals.

In addition, there is sexual harassment. Harassment can involve actions in which employment decisions are contingent on an employee providing sexual favors—this form of harassment is labeled quid pro quo. Another form of harassment is called hostile work environment, which can involve rude jokes, offensive sexual images, or other behaviors that sexualize a work environment.

Finally, there is retaliation. This is a form of discrimination that occurs in response to employees trying to assert their rights to a workplace that is free from discrimination and/or harassment. As the U.S. Equal Employment Opportunity Commission (EEOC) reports,[2] it is illegal to retaliate against employees who file or serve as a witness in EEOC activities, discuss discrimination with a superordinate, refuse to engage in discrimination, refuse sexual advances or intervene to help others experiencing unwanted sexual attention, and/or request reasonable accommodations.

All of these types of overt discrimination are illegal. Although discrimination is supposed to be regulated by the EEOC, the office handles only a fraction of discrimination cases. This is apparent in the process data. In 2018, despite receiving 554,000 calls and emails, the EEOC handled only 200,000 cases and then confirmed that only 76,418 cases were legitimate. This means that only 13% of the cases reported were confirmed. One issue is that the agency does not have enough resources—controlling for inflation, it had a much smaller budget in 2020 than it did in 1980. It also had 42% less staff in 2020 than in 1980, despite a 50% increase in the labor force. And throughout a portion of Trump's presidency and until Biden's election, three of the five commissioner seats remained vacant.

Another major issue is that discrimination is vastly underreported. People generally (a) do not want to see themselves as targets or

---

[2] U.S. Equal Employment Opportunity Commission. (2022). *Facts about retaliation.* https://www.eeoc.gov/facts-about-retaliation.

victims of discrimination and (b) do not want to engage in the protracted conflict that can arise if a formal complaint were raised. A very common reaction to discrimination claims is disbelief. Being a target of discrimination can feel disempowering, can open people up to scrutiny and criticism, and can result in a variety of forms of retaliation. It follows that the 554,000 calls to the EEOC in 2018 reflect a small fraction of the number of discriminatory experiences that people encounter at work.

Importantly, however, when the 13% of the cases do get prosecuted, the settlements can be enormous. Here are some of the eye-popping examples: $240 million from Hill County Farms, $192 million from Coca-Cola, and $132 million from Shoney's. In short, overt discrimination is illegal, but it is still a problem and can be very costly to organizations.

Subtle Discrimination

When people think about discrimination, they often think about overt types of discrimination. However, we believe it is very important to also recognize a second form of bias—subtle discrimination. Laws restrict the extent to which organizations can overtly discriminate, but what about more subtle forms? Subtle discrimination is sometimes labeled unconscious bias, everyday bias, or microaggressions. We use the term subtle discrimination as an umbrella label to incorporate each of these ways of thinking about behavioral acts of bias that are ambiguous, difficult to detect, low in intensity, and often unintentional.[3]

To get a sense of what subtle discrimination can look like, think about a person you don't like very much. Now, imagine that you're walking down the hall and this person is walking toward you. How do you behave? Sometimes we fold our arms. Sometimes we try to

---

[3] Jones, K. P., Peddie, C. I., Gilrane, V. L., King, E. B., & Gray, A. L. (2016). Not so subtle: A meta-analytic investigation of the correlates of subtle and overt discrimination. *Journal of Management*, 42(6), 1588–1613.

avoid the person. We don't look them in the eye. We don't really smile. Sometimes we say a quick, quiet hello. And sometimes, we get on our phone and pretend like we're distracted by a call. When these types of behaviors are directed toward people because of their identity, this is subtle discrimination.

In 2019, Procter & Gamble created a film (available on YouTube)[4] that depicts such discrimination from the point of view of a Black man. Car windows are raised, an elevator door closes, restaurant tables are chosen, and security guards' gazes are sharpened in response to the protagonist. These everyday acts of racism reflect pernicious forms of discrimination.

A total of 46 of the 50 MBA students reported that they had experienced subtle types of discrimination. For instance, one Black professional wrote,

> Right after one of these police killings of an unarmed Black persons, my manager brought in a big Trump flag and hung it in the room where we have our daily meetings. I was the only Black person on that project.

An Asian MBA student reflected,

> Throughout my whole education, people assume that I'm good at math and make remarks about like, "Oh wow, you must have done really well on the SAT. Oh, you must be really good at math!" But, I am NOT good at math (which is why I ended up in science) and I did NOT do well on my SAT (at least not well given my school ranking at the time). These indirect "compliments" actually fed into my imposter syndrome even more because I felt like I wasn't meeting societal expectations of what an "Asian" should represent.

Another member of the class explained,

> Yes, during an interview there were subtle biases such as fake half smiles, pre-COVID not shaking my hand afterwards which all the other

---

[4] Procter & Gamble. (2019). *The look*. https://www.youtube.com/watch?v=bxZBtWGYV1c.

interviewers did, and having almost a cold personality as if they didn't believe I belonged there or I was too young to hold that position. The discrimination was evident when I saw them engage with their own staff compared to myself that it was subtly different.

In organizations, these behaviors happen in interpersonal encounters at water coolers, in virtual meetings, and in job interviews. Subtle discrimination can also emerge in written form, such as performance evaluations and letters of recommendation. Indeed, a great deal of the research that we have conducted focuses on subtle discrimination across the employment cycle. Before we discuss specific manifestations of subtle bias at different phases of employment, we provide more illustrations of these experiences through our MBA students' responses to the question, "How have you experienced subtle bias in organizations, if at all?":

- "I look very young, and people often don't take me seriously. They think I'm not professional."
- "Male colleagues saying things like, 'You have the best handwriting, so you write for us.'"
- "People questioning my math [as a woman]."
- "People assume that, as a woman, I'm an event organizer not an investor."
- "'#Metoo' fears that prevent me from having access to male leaders because they are afraid."
- "Male coworkers often interrupt me in group settings."
- "When I worked as a manager, people would rudely and dismissively ask me if they could speak to the manager. I saw how differently (much 'less importantly') I was treated when they discovered I was the person they wanted to speak with."
- "I will be ignored or disregarded, and a man will say the EXACT same thing, and it will be perceived differently/accepted!"
- "People were dismissive when I spoke sometimes during meetings and would cut me off, clearly not caring about my thoughts or intentions."

- "There are undertones in the way the person says or phrases their response (e.g., dismissive tones and smirks)."
- "Patients would expect me [as a woman] to be more caring and to stay in conversations longer about their feelings. They also overtly flirt with me and say inappropriate things such as 'You're a perfect porcelain doll,' and 'I love how submissive you are.'"
- "Was told my lack of contract extension was not due to my solid performance, but that I acted entitled. Said I [as a woman] should consider being more feminine."
- "The small things people say as jokes."
- "Comments about my female boss being ugly and how she shouldn't be the image of training programs."
- "In the military, those who are screaming and harsh are judged as 'bitchy' if they are female, but are judged as good leaders if they are male."
- "When recruiting for engineering positions, I found that it was very hard to be taken seriously when I was dressed more feminine. I cut my hair like a boy and was immediately considered for positions."
- "I [as a man] received more candid feedback from our supervisor than did my female colleague. As a result, she struggled to understand what she needed to do to improve her performance."
- "I was mistaken for the cleaning staff."
- "People often ask me [a Hispanic man]: 'Do you like spicy food?' 'What do you think of uneducated Hispanics?' 'Would you ever marry a White girl?'"

Subtle Discrimination in Getting the Interview

Before they can get a job, people usually have to first get an interview. Our research shows that subtle discrimination—as manifested both in face-to-face interactions and in written text—can prevent people from marginalized backgrounds from getting an interview. Some of our most impactful research has examined the experiences that people encounter when they submit job applications in retail stores. In this research, ostensible job applicants who are also trained research assistants go into stores that have advertised open positions. They ask to speak to the store manager and then ask that person a few questions about the application and job. We are interested in the store manager's behavior in terms of the length of the conversation; the number of words spoken; and negativity toward the job applicant in terms of avoiding eye contact, rudeness, hostility, and a lack of enthusiasm. The ostensible job applicants provide their observations of these behaviors on surveys, and we code audio recordings of the conversations for these behaviors (which is legal in the states where this research is conducted).

The results of our research using this real-world paradigm provide convincing evidence that subtle discrimination emerges toward a variety of stereotyped groups. People were treated more negatively when they were wearing prostheses that made them appear to be obese (a fat suit) or pregnant (a pregnancy belly) than when they did not. People encountered more negative reactions when they wore a hat that said "Gay and Proud" than when they wore a hat that said "Texan and Proud." Women reported more subtle discrimination when they wore a hijab that made them appear to be Muslim than when they did not. Together, these data suggest that even before they get a formal interview, people from marginalized backgrounds are experiencing subtle discrimination from people in positions of power.

Subtle bias also emerges in terms of differences in the way that recommendation letters are written for people from different backgrounds. This research[5,6] shows that letters for women tend to be shorter, which is a heuristic for a weaker letter. These letters tend to include more words and phrases that emphasize warmth, such as

---

[5] Hebl, M., Nittrouer, C. L., Corrington, A. R., & Madera, J. M. (2018, September). How we describe male and female job applicants differently. *Harvard Business Review.*
[6] Madera, J., Hebl, M., & Martin, R. (2009). Gender and letters of recommendation for academics: Agentic and communal differences. *Journal of Applied Psychology, 94,* 1591–1599.

"she's caring" or "she's sensitive." This subtle reminder of the warmth stereotype is particularly problematic because being warm is generally viewed as inconsistent with the characteristics that are necessary for many high-level positions.

Letters of recommendation for women also tend to include more phrases that raise doubt about competence than do letters for men.[7] Examples of doubt-raisers are phrases such as "she has the potential to be good" or "she might be one of your best" rather than the clear expectation that "he will be good" or "he will be one of your best." Even this seemingly small, nuanced difference in the descriptions of male and female candidates can make a difference in who gets invited for an interview.

Subtle Discrimination in the Interview

Once applicants get through the first hurdle and make it to the interview, they can run into additional forms of subtle discrimination. Interviewer biases can include a variety of stereotypes and prejudices, but one overarching bias is *the similarity effect*. People tend to prefer, and tend to hire, others who are similar to them—people who have had the same training, people who went to the same college, or people who are in some other way very similar. Sometimes, employers rationalize favoring similar others by claiming that such individuals are just "a good fit." This is often a code word for bias. Appearance-based biases can also influence interviewers who have a sense of "the right look" for a particular job. What does a "good applicant" look like? Appearance-based stereotypes suggest that tall, White, slender, well-dressed people in conservative business attire are considered "good." These biases translate into different behaviors toward interviewees.

In interviews, verbal and nonverbal behaviors carry a lot of weight. And interviewers might give off the cues of warmth,

---

[7] Madera, J., Hebl, M., Valian, V., Martin, R., & Dial, H. (2019). Raising doubt in letters of recommendation for prospective faculty: Gender differences and their impact. *Journal of Business and Psychology, 34*(3), 287–303.

acceptance, and rapport. They may laugh more, encourage, or ask applicants for follow-ups to their responses, and that warmth or indication of interest can increase applicants' comfort, confidence, and performance. In the absence of that favorable treatment, and in the absence of that rapport, applicants do not feel as reinforced, and they may perform more poorly. You can generally tell when you are interacting with a person whether or not they are interested in you; so too can applicants.

Applicants themselves place differential amounts of attention to verbal and nonverbal cues. For instance, research has examined how White and Black applicants describe their interview experiences. White applicants tend to believe that their interviews went pretty well, that they said the right things, and that they had a good conversation with the interviewer. Black applicants' observations tend to reflect more on specific behaviors—verbal and nonverbal—suggesting that they don't (can't) trust the words that are spoken.

Together, these patterns create a self-fulfilling prophecy. Interviewers have biases against applicants from marginalized backgrounds and treat them differently than others during interviews. People from marginalized backgrounds notice these differences and can feel and even perform worse in the interviews, thereby confirming the interviewers' biases that created the differences in the first place.[8] This pattern is hugely problematic, and it is all a manifestation of subtle bias.

Subtle Discrimination in Performance Management and Development

Success in an organization can be fostered through high-quality feedback and through developmental opportunities. Unfortunately, evidence suggests that both feedback and development are affected

---

[8] Word, C. O., Zanna, M. P., & Cooper, J. (1974). The nonverbal mediation of self-fulfilling prophecies in interracial interaction. *Journal of Experimental Social Psychology*, 10(2), 109–120.

by biases. In our own research, we examined the kinds of developmental opportunities that men and women in health care organizations and in the oil and gas industry received.[9] The results showed that women had less access to challenging work experiences than men and that managers were less likely to give women challenging opportunities. This is a critical loss because being challenged is necessary for building new knowledge, skills, and abilities.

We also found that managers tended to withhold negative feedback from women; they avoided talking about negative issues and focused on positive ones. This may seem nice, but like challenging assignments, negative feedback is necessary for understanding and building on opportunities for growth. Indeed, when we asked men and women whether they wanted to take on challenging work activities and whether they appreciated negative feedback, there were no gender differences. The differences in development are due to managers' stereotypes, not actual differences in men and women. This means that subtle biases about women are getting in the way of their learning and development, and in turn, they may not have the opportunity to develop the competencies needed to be promoted into (or to be successful in) leadership positions.

Subtle Discrimination in Promotion to Leadership

When we think about leaders, we picture a White man. He's probably wearing professional clothes, and he's probably relatively attractive and not too old. But he's definitely White, and he's definitely male. These expectations of what a leader "is" get in the way of anyone else becoming a leader. There are inconsistencies between this leader prototype and stereotypes of White women and people of color. These inconsistencies make it difficult for White women and

---

[9] King, E. B., Botsford, W. E., Hebl, M., Kazama, S., Perkins, A., & Dawson, J. (2012). Benevolent sexism at work: Gender differences in the distribution of challenging developmental experiences. *Journal of Management, 38*, 1835–1866.

people of color to be recognized, promoted, and positioned as powerful leaders.

Much of the evidence on these challenges has focused on the underrepresentation of women in positions of leadership. According to a report by Catalyst, in 2023,[10] there were 41 female chief executive officers of S&P companies—8.2%.[11] This is far short of equal representation, since women make up more than half of the workforce. One of the barriers standing in the way of women's ascension to leadership is stereotypes. Women are stereotyped as being warm, sincere, and kind—characteristics that are generally incongruent with expectations of leaders. Leaders are expected to be assertive and authoritative, not kind and sensitive. Of course, these stereotypes are even more incongruent in fields that are dominated by men.

One of our female MBA students reported the difficulty she had in getting people to listen to her. She stated,

> I specifically put myself in a group with all males to prepare myself for my career switch into investment banking. During our group meetings, I found that I always had to defend every word I said, but when a male said something, they did not have to go into deep analysis as to why. For example, we were building a financial model and had to decide a growth rate for our sales projections. A couple of men wanted to choose a growth rate that was wrong, and the other men in the group wanted to go with it. I gave examples of why the growth rate was not a good choice. The men refused to back down, so I brought up a tool that provided robust data to show that my growth rate was the better one to use for the model. After showing the data, the men decided that my growth rate was a better growth rate for the model. I was so mad about this because I did not understand why my qualitative reasoning was not enough to win them over. Other men said things and did not have to go in depth like I did to get buy in. I do not think they did this to be malicious, but it just shows the bias that resides in men toward women, specifically in male dominated fields.

---

[10] https://www.catalyst.org/research/women-ceos-of-the-sp-500/
[11] *Women CEOs of the S&P 500*. (2023, February 3). Catalyst.

One quick and easy way to see the challenges that female leaders have is to look at popular self-help books that depict the nuanced experiences of potential female leaders. Women learn from these books that they should "Lead Like a Girl,"[12,13] lead "Gracefully,"[14] "Pitch Like a Girl,"[15] and "Lean In"[16] but should also avoid "Mean Girls at Work"[17] and "Taming Your Alpha Bitch."[18] These titles reflect the thin line women walk between being seen as too nice and being seen as too bitchy to lead, and they also reflect the subtle messages that women often encounter about their leadership potential.

Subtle discrimination extends beyond sexism. For example, mounting evidence shows that despite the fact that Asian Americans outperform members of other racial groups in terms of education, income, and employment metrics, they are least likely to be promoted to management positions.[19,20] This phenomenon has commonly been referred to as the bamboo ceiling. The underlying stereotype of Asian Americans is that they are high in competence but not high in likability, and this combination is incongruent with our cultural stereotypes of what it means to be a good leader. These stereotypes can, of course, be wildly inaccurate. In addition, the Eastern values that many Asian Americans subscribe to tend to emphasize deference to authority and humility—characteristics that are incongruent with the more U.S. leadership stereotypes, which more commonly ascribe to Western values such as self-promotion and ability to command. And so, Asian people are not promoted.

---

[12] Banks, J. (2021). *Lead like a girl: A guide to successful female leadership* (B09NH3NW46).
[13] Feldheim, D. (2022). *Dare to lead like a girl: How to survive and thrive in the corporate jungle*. Rowman & Littlefield.
[14] Tallon, M. S. (2016). *Leading gracefully: A woman's guide to confident, authentic, and effective leadership*. Highest Path.
[15] Lichtenberg, R. (2006). *Pitch like a girl: Get respected, get noticed, get what you want*. Rodale.
[16] Sandberg, S. (2013). *Lean in: Women, work, and the will to lead*. Knopf.
[17] Crowley, K., & Elster, K. (2013). *Mean girls at work: How to stay professional when things get personal*. McGraw Hill.
[18] Grado, R., & Whitman, C. (2012). *Taming your alpha bitch: How to be fierce and feminine (and get everything you want!)*. Penguin.
[19] Gee, B., & Peck, D. (2018, May) Asian Americans are the least likely group in the U.S. to be promoted to management. *Harvard Business Review*.
[20] Johnson, S. K., & Sy, T. (2016, December 19). Why aren't there more Asian Americans in leadership positions? *Harvard Business Review*.

But if It's Subtle, It's Not So Bad, Right?

Wrong. Subtle discrimination is just as bad, if not worse, than overt discrimination. Indeed, we examined more than 40 different studies that measured the effects of each form of discrimination on outcomes such as psychological well-being, job satisfaction, turnover, and performance. Across these outcomes, the effects of subtle discrimination were just as negative (if not worse) than those of overt discrimination.

Why? One reason that subtle discrimination is particularly problematic is that it is difficult for targets to know whether or not they did something to deserve the negative experiences they encountered. If someone says, "We think women are incompetent and don't hire them," then a female job applicant knows that she did not personally do anything wrong. She can attribute the negative treatment she encountered in an interview to the biases of the interviewers. But if instead, she gets some ambiguous cues that maybe the interviewer does not really think the job is a good fit for her, the job applicant would not know whether she lacked qualifications, had a bad interview, or otherwise messed up. This ambiguity in the attribution could be stressful, and trying to understand and interpret the experience could be cognitively taxing. Every moment the job applicant spends trying to understand if and how she did something wrong could undermine her well-being and confidence. It is clear that subtle discrimination is indeed both prevalent and problematic in contemporary organizations.

Tools for Working Together

1. Reflect on the overt forms of discrimination that you have experienced or witnessed in the workplace. Who discriminated against whom? What did the discrimination look like? And what was the consequence of the discrimination?
2. Reflect on more subtle forms of discrimination that you have experienced or witnessed in the workplace. What did this

behavior look like, and what were the resulting consequences? Do you think the examples of subtle discrimination were more, less, or just as pernicious as those of overt discrimination?
3. What are some of the reasons people might engage in more subtle discrimination rather than overt discrimination?
4. What might you do to raise awareness of more subtle forms of discrimination?

8

Organization-Level Discrimination

Van Heusen advertises itself as having "the best-selling shirt brand in the world" and men's (and women's) dress clothes that are "made simple and smart" (Figure 8.1). Indeed, this brand has spanned more than 140 years of innovative design. In 2021, PVH Corp. (formerly called Phillips-Van Heusen Corporation)[1] had an impressive net revenue of $9.8 billion and a 2021 (July) marketing strategy that depicted a White woman and Black man modeling clothes on the home page, in addition to a 100% pledge to recruit and source ethically, promote safe workplaces, amplify worker's voices, empower women, and foster inclusion and diversity.

What a long way Van Heusen had come. An examination of a vintage 1950s ad depicts one of the most racist and disturbing images that we have ever seen in advertising (Figure 8.2).[2] It is a Van Heusen ad glorifying White people for their choice in Van Heusen shirts and mocking a non-White person.

One would expect all advertising is now free of such shocking depictions of racism given that so many organizations have hired diversity, equity, and inclusion (DEI) officers; created mission statements that promote and promise diversity; and instituted other policies to create fair and equitable workplaces for others. However, in 2016, a report revealed that Facebook was letting advertisers exclude Black, Hispanic, and individuals from other marginalized backgrounds from seeing ads.[3] Furthermore, at the end of 2021, Van

---

[1] https://en.wikipedia.org/wiki/PVH_(company).
[2] Helpern, W. (2016, April 17). 18 awful vintage ads from the 20th century that show how far we have progressed. *Business Insider*. https://www.businessinsider.com/vintage-sexist-and-racist-ads-2016-4#van-heusen-mocked-at-nonwhite-people-in-the-1950s-9.
[3] Angwin, J., & Parris, T., Jr. (2016, October 28). *Facebook lets advertisers exclude users by race*. Propublica. https://www.propublica.org/article/facebook-lets-advertisers-exclude-users-by-race.

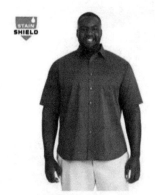 

Essential Stain Shield Woven Solid Short Sleeve Shirt Regular Fit - Big & Tall

Essential Stain Shield Plaid Print Short Sleeve Shirt Slim Fit
$55.00

Figure 8.1 Modern Van Heusen clothing models.
Source: Phillips-Van Heusen Corporation. https://www.vanheusen.com/collections/shirts-1.

Heusen was sold to Authentic Brands Group LLC. Gone were the oaths to empowering diversity, and the website went back to predominantly featuring White men.

In fact, Propublica purchased an ad for Facebook's housing categories and was asked to indicate detailed inclusion and exclusion targets. Excluding people on the basis of race, or explicitly limiting the information available to people from particular racial backgrounds, was an option. Three years later (March 2019), the giant network Facebook settled five lawsuits that claimed the company allowed many companies to illegally advertise not only home sales but also job opportunities. Some opportunities would only be visible to men, younger people, and those living in White neighborhoods. Facebook's own job ads that it posted screened out older users. An audit in 2021 suggests Facebook may continue to use discriminatory algorithms that restrict people from marginalized backgrounds.[4]

---

[4] Hao, K. (2021, April 9). Facebook's ad algorithms are still excluding women from seeing jobs. *MIT Technology Review*. https://www.technologyreview.com/2021/04/09/1022217/

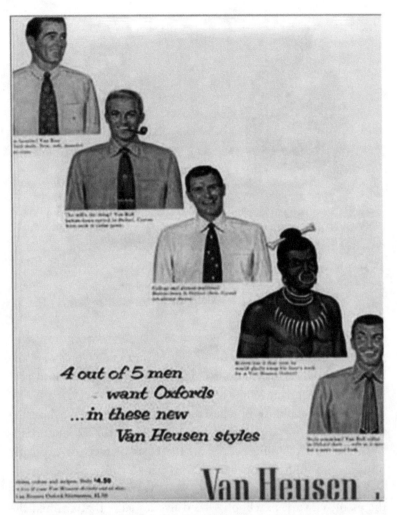

Figure 8.2 1950s Van Heusen racist advertisement.

Restrictions of product marketing (e.g., Van Heusen shirts) and product information (e.g., Facebook) are clearly problematic from a social perspective, but it is particularly worrisome that restrictions also apply to employment opportunities. Organizational biases can

facebook-ad-algorithm-sex-discrimination.

manifest structurally as policies or practices that restrict job ads to people from particular backgrounds (as Facebook seems to have done) or that describe jobs in ways that are either purposely or unknowingly racist, sexist, ageist, heterosexist, or otherwise exclusive. These are examples of *organizational biases*—policies, practices, or procedures that favor people from one group over people from another group. Organizational biases reflect historical systems of oppression and advantage, as well as individual biases that are baked into how things get done. These biases are exemplified across the employment cycle, from application to promotion.

Organizational Biases in Getting the Job

Getting a job can be difficult, particularly because most job openings are not published publicly on job sites and there are often an overwhelming number of applications.[5] Instead, most jobs are still acquired through personal or professional connections, which is problematic because there exist stark inequities in the extent to which people have access to networks. If recruitment procedures take this approach and hiring managers reach out to people who are already in their social networks, the applicant pool will largely be composed of people who are similar to the hiring managers—our networks are typically composed of people who are similar to us.

Narrow recruitment strategies reflect and perpetuate organizational biases. If a company's policy is to only attend or to prioritize job fairs at Ivy League colleges, its potential applicant pool will be limited to people who have had access to rare (and costly) educational opportunities. Thus, biases can emerge through organizational recruitment policies and practices that directly impact the diversity of potential applicants.

---

[5] See Freeland Fisher, J. (2019, December 27). *How to get a job often comes down to one elite personal asset, and many people still don't realize it.* CNBC. https://www.cnbc.com/2019/12/27/how-to-get-a-job-often-comes-down-to-one-elite-personal-asset.html.

Organizational Biases in Compensation

Biases also have a huge impact on compensation. Would you be surprised to learn that math professors tend to make higher salaries than English professors? Even with the same level of education and experience, at the same institutions, and even with the same kind of productivity expectations, these positions are paid quite differently. According to salary.com, English professors earn on average $95,000 per year, whereas math professors average $105,000 per year. Although there may be potential explanations for this gap in pay, it is useful to note that the representation of women and people of color is substantially lower in math departments than in English departments. Unfortunately, systematic differences in compensation between fields often coincide with the representation of people from marginalized groups.

These systemic issues are exacerbated by structural factors. One structural characteristic that can make pay inequity even worse is that past compensation can be used to determine future compensation. An employer may ask a job applicant how much they were paid at their previous position and use that amount as an anchor for their job offer. This practice can result in the perpetuation of inequity across jobs and organizations.

Another structural issue that can exacerbate pay inequity is hidden or invisible compensation systems. It is impossible for people to evaluate the fairness of their compensation relative to others in their organizations if they do not know and cannot find out others' compensation. By hiding pay levels, employees are disempowered.

Finally, it is worth noting that salary differences compound over time. Factoring performance- and cost-of-living-based percentage increases in salary for jobs that vary over the many years of a career can dramatically affect one's financial situation. What starts out as seemingly small differences in salary accumulate over time because raises and bonuses are often proportional to one's starting salary. Molehills do indeed become mountains.[6]

---

[6] Valian, V. (1999). *Why so slow? The advancement of women.* MIT Press.

Organizational Biases in Promotion

You open your email, ready to start the day. Waiting for you is a message with a phrase such as "We are happy to share the news . . ." or "Join us in welcoming . . . ." This message informs you that John Smith has been promoted and (surprise!) is now your boss. This has happened to each of the authors on multiple occasions, and we bet it has happened or will happen to you.

Promotions are often surprising because the decisions that guide them tend to happen (a) behind closed doors, (b) based on unclear criteria, (c) and with lots of room for bias. The processes and procedures that underlie promotion decisions reflect forms of organizational biases. Consistent with this, organizational scholars have described the potential for bias in promotion decisions as likely because

> promotions to mid- and upper-level management positions require decision makers to assess individuals in uncertain and complex environments. Such judgements are inherently subjective because of the difficulty of determining the performance of a single individual in the context of interdependent jobs, complex relationships, ambiguous problem situations, and extended time frames. (p. 12)[7]

Some of the organizational biases are readily evident in the field of academia, where it is relatively easy to turn our research attention inward to matters within our own Ivory Tower. A review summarizes the many biases that women face in the field.[8] Specifically, compared to men, women face more impediments to career advancement, they are not given the same financial compensation, they are assigned

---

[7] Ruderman, M. N., Ohlott, P. J., & Kram, K. E. (1995). Promotion decisions as a diversity practice. *Journal of Management Development, 14*(2), 6–23. https://doi.org/10.1108/02621719510078867.

[8] Gruber, J., Mendle, J., Lindquist, K. A., Schmader, T., Clark, L. A., Bliss-Moreau, E., Akinola, M., Atlas, L., Barch, D., Barrett, L., Borelli, J., Brannon, T., Bunge, S., Campos, B., Cantlon, J., Carter, R., Carter Sowell, A., Chen, S., Craske, M., . . . Williams, L. A. (2021). The future of women in psychological science. *Perspectives on Psychological Science, 16*(3), 483–516.

different service opportunities that have implications for promotion, there is considerable work–family conflict, they hold lower and fewer positions of power, they face harassment and incivility, they are less self-promoting, and they face more issues of belongingness. Moreover, it is often more difficult for those at the intersection of two marginalized identities (e.g., being a woman and from a marginalized racial group).

Not surprisingly, these biases that women face in academia are the same ones that they face in other organizations. In our research,[9] we identified one perhaps subtle way in which academia may be biased against women. We noticed that more men seemed to be invited to give formal presentations than women. These formal presentations—colloquium talks—are important in academia because they allow faculty to present their research, make connections, learn about the latest cross-cutting research, gain collaborators, and refine their ideas. Even more important, colloquium talks are often the gateway to being considered for jobs and are sometimes informal interviews. We wondered if the gender difference we noted was evident throughout the United States. So, we looked at the colloquium talks that faculty members gave across six different disciplines at the top 50 universities in the country. Men were invited more often than women across the board. It was not because there are just more male than female professors. It was not because male professors tend to be older and/or more senior in their fields. It was not because women declined invitations more, and it was not because women did not believe that it was not important to give colloquium talks. It was because the colloquium speakers were choosing men over women, and this finding was exacerbated when men were the colloquium chairs who did the speaker selection.

As an example of a formal type of organizational bias, if an organization requires a particular experience (e.g., international placement) or certificate that is less accessible to some employees than

---

[9] Nittrouer, C. L., Hebl, M. R., Trump-Steele, R., Ashburn-Nardo, L., Lane, D., & Valian, V. (2018). Gender bias in colloquium speakers. *Proceedings of the National Academy of Sciences of the USA*, 115(1), 104–108.

others, this will ultimately prohibit some employees from even being eligible for the promotion. A more subtle type of organizational bias includes promotions that are structured to be based on nominations or recommendations[10] that will be influenced by all of the individual-level biases mentioned in Chapter 7. Unfortunately, these types of biases are often baked into the way things get done in organizations—decision-makers may believe that they should promote the person with whom they would feel comfortable having a beer rather than the person who would do best in the job. So the organizational processes that are set up to make promotion decisions are often subjective and obscure, allowing individual biases to manifest.

Conclusion

This brief overview of the kinds of biases that exist at the level of the organization supplements our description of individuals' biases. These are complementary, mutually reinforcing phenomena that are barriers to DEI. Thus, in Section 3, we move beyond describing the problems of individual and organizational biases toward potential strategies to begin working together to create and sustain DEI.

Tools for Working Together

Consider the organizational-level biases that your organizations may be displaying, whether intentionally or unintentionally.

1. How does your organization fill its positions? Are there company requirements about posting jobs? How might your organization's processes give rise to biases from social connections in the workforce that you hire? What formal

---

[10] The kind where a leader asks their friends who should be promoted.

procedures do you think might be adopted to avoid these biases?
2. How does your organization currently depict people on its web pages, materials, and advertisements? Does the diversity that appears reflect the diversity that actually exists in the company? What could be done to better showcase your organization?
3. How does your organization ensure that there are not gender or racial inequities in pay? Is there pay transparency? If not, are salary studies conducted within your organization? How might you encourage your organization to do this?

SECTION 3
STRATEGIES TO HELP US WORK TOGETHER

Here's a shocking statistic: Less than 1% of certified public accountants (CPAs) in the United States are Black.[1] One individual making up this bleak percentage is Professor Adrian Mayse, who wrote a clever, well-illustrated children's book titled *When I Grow Up, I Want to Be an . . . Accountant*.[2] When Mayse was a child, however, he did not want to be an accountant. The only accountants he knew growing up were White, so he didn't identify with the profession as one for him or one that he could do. In fact, it wasn't until later in college when he saw another Black accountant that he began to consider the career. The current landscape of individuals holding a bachelor's degrees in accounting reveals that 60% identify as White, 13% identify as Hispanic/Latino, and 7% identify as Black/African American.[3] A survey examining why so few Black and Hispanic individuals who have taken at least one class or been otherwise exposed to some accounting do not pursue it professionally thereafter reveals that these individuals perceive it to be a career

---

[1] Gonzalez, A. (2020, December 4). *Number of the day: 1%*. https://www.goingconcern.com/number-of-the-day-1.

[2] Mayse, A. L. (2021). *When I grow up I want to be . . . an accountant*.

[3] Association of International Certified Professional Accountants. (2022). *2021 trends: A report on accounting education, the CPA exam, and public accounting firms' hiring of recent graduates*. https://micpa.org/docs/site/educator-assets/2021-trends-report.pdf?sfvrsn=bfb9c261_2.

that is unfulfilling, do not feel passionate about it, or have financial hesitations related to gaining CPA licensure.[4]

Where there are gross racial or other social inequities in the distribution of people in esteemed societal positions or organizations as a whole, how should we as individuals (targets and allies) and organizations, more generally, respond?

The accounting profession has responded to this scarcity in numbers by making bold moves to increase diversity.[5] These involve individual change, such as having specific individuals serving as role models (helping others learn more about and consider accounting careers), becoming an ambassador (getting the word out to students about the field of public accounting and how exciting and lucrative it can be), providing summer internships (hiring a younger person to get firsthand experience in a field of accounting), and providing exemplars of other accountants who are Black and/or Hispanic. But the profession as a whole is also taking action, spending more than $470 million to bring diverse talent to the field.[6] The Center for Audit Quality is partnering with the National Association of Black Accountants (NABA, Inc.) to help Black community college members transfer into 4-year Black academic institutions to study accounting. They developed partnerships with a number of mentors, tutoring services, and other resources; and they have worked on developing a social media campaign targeted at younger, diverse audiences.[7]

More generally, the absence, restriction, or stigmatization of certain groups in particular organizations or levels in an organization require more of both an individual and a collective, organizational action. In 1988, two contemporary singers (although from

---

[4] Center for Audit Quality. (2022, January). *Increasing diversity in the accounting profession pipeline: Challenges and opportunities*. https://www.thecaq.org/increasing-diversity-in-the-accounting-profession-pipeline.

[5] Center for Audit Quality. (2022, August 22). The accounting profession is making bold moves to increase diversity. *CFODive*. https://www.cfodive.com/spons/the-accounting-profession-is-making-bold-moves-to-increase-diversity/629627.

[6] Center for Audit Quality. (2022, August 22). The accounting profession is making bold moves to increase diversity. *CFODive*. https://www.cfodive.com/spons/the-accounting-profession-is-making-bold-moves-to-increase-diversity/629627.

[7] https://www.joinaccountingplus.com.

very different genres) released songs about the vast financial wage disparities that exist between groups of people in the United States, and the lyrics of each song offer solutions that focus on very different sets of actions. In the "Man in the Mirror," Michael Jackson sings about the necessity of individual action—we must start by examining ourselves, by looking at the man in the mirror. In "Talkin' Bout a Revolution," Tracy Chapman sings about collective action. In this section of the book, we discuss different solutions to inequity and ways that individuals, allies, and organizations can work together to reduce discrimination and create more harmonious workplaces.

It is perhaps never so timely to be writing about the need for both individual and collective/organizational actions, given the racial reckoning that was instigated in the United States by highly publicized, senseless murders of Black people at the hands of police officers and the emerging legislative efforts to eliminate DEI initiatives in higher education. The racial reckoning calls each of us to look at ourselves and identify and consider the racist behaviors in ourselves. That task feels very uncomfortable for many people, and many experience cognitive dissonance—a discomfort that is caused when people's attitudes ("I'm a good person and I try to treat people equally") are misaligned with their actual behaviors ("I have done racist things"). The racial reckoning compels us to sit with that dissonance and own it, to consider our failings, and to think about how we can become better people. But this is a very difficult task for most people because, as we learn from some of the earliest psychology lessons, humans strive to maintain positive self-esteem, to think of themselves as the protagonist in most situations, and to take credit for successes and blame others or situations for shortcomings. These tendencies are at odds with the racial reckoning. Sometimes we have acted in racist ways, we have initiated and maintained difficult interactions or relationships with others who are different just because they are different. This acknowledgment is necessary and a precursor to being able to successfully work with diverse groups of others, but it is difficult to own that you might be and probably are part of the problem.

The racial reckoning also calls us to engage—as targets, as allies, and as institutions—in collective action. To stand up and support others who similarly stand up. And it is these actions that we particularly focus on in this section. What can targets, allies, and organizations do to reduce the biases that affect their workplaces?

9
What Can Individual Targets of Discrimination Do?

In the 1980s, a woman named Ann was working at one of the four big major accounting firms and was trying to become a partner. In the 5 years that she worked at the firm, she was exceptionally successful and won some of the firm's largest contracts worth an estimated $34–$44 million—numbers significantly higher than those of any of the 87 male workers who were also trying to become partners.[1] Her clients and peers described her as having strong leadership qualities, good business sense, and outstanding communication skills. A total of 62 of the 88 workers were promoted to partner, but shockingly, Ann was not one of them. Despite some ardent supporters, other partners voting on the decision rejected her, stating that she needed to take a "course in charm school," "is a lady using foul language," and was "macho." One of her biggest supporters (yes, supporters!) advised her to "walk more femininely, talk more femininely, dress more femininely, wear makeup and jewelry. Have your hair styled."[2]

There is no doubt that Ann is not the only woman in history working in a male-dominated organization who has experienced this situation or some similarly extremely unfair version of it. But in Ann's words, "The only thing that makes me remarkable is that I happened to stand up for a particular principle at a particular time."[3]

---

[1] *Ann B. Hopkins, Appellant, v. Price Waterhouse.ann B. Hopkins v. Price Waterhouse, Appellant*, 825 F.2d 458 (D.C. Cir. 1987). https://law.justia.com/cases/federal/appellate-courts/F2/825/458/450279.

[2] C-SPAN. (1989, May 5). *Price Waterhouse v. Ann B. Hopkins* [Video]. https://www.c-span.org/video/?7373-1/price-waterhouse-v-ann-b-hopkins.

[3] Barnes, B. (2018, July 17). Ann Hopkins, winner of a workplace bias fight, dies at 74. *The New York Times*. https://www.wral.com/ann-hopkins-winner-of-a-workplace-bias-fight-dies-at-74/17704684.

Ann Hopkins was the plaintiff in one of the most famous workplace discrimination cases (*Ann B. Hopkins v. Price Waterhouse*, 1987). She believed that being passed over for the partner position was unjust and boldly challenged the decision by speaking up and hiring lawyers. She won her case, a decision that not only historically expanded laws on workplace discrimination (Title VII) to include gender discrimination but also paved the way for the modern-day extension of protecting employees who are LGBTQ.

There are many reasons why other targets of discrimination do *not* speak up and hire lawyers in response. Some do not possess the objective evidence. As we have discussed, discrimination is often more subtle, interpersonal, and sometimes even unintentional. For Hopkins, however, there were significant paper trails and people who testified on her behalf. Other targets may not speak up because they worry about retaliation and losing their jobs. An operator of ambulance services in Tennessee was found to have violated federal law[4] when supervisors and upper management failed to stop the sexual harassment that was directed toward several female paramedics. When a female paramedic complained about the sexually hostile work environment, the company retaliated by firing her. Others might not have the resources (financial or emotional) to engage in a prolonged response to discrimination. This chapter identifies potentially simpler strategies that individuals can adopt. They are based on empirical work that has shown them to be effective, at least in some situations and contexts. They may not have the boldness of action that Hopkins exhibited, but they do provide alternatives for action that the targets themselves can adopt should they desire to do so.

We believe there are overarching steps to reducing the biases that exist in organizations. The first one is to be aware of the biases. Awareness is critical. If we aren't willing to accept that we have or that our organization has biases, there isn't much hope for change. As Eric Yuan, founder and chief executive officer of Zoom states,

---

[4] U.S. Equal Employment Opportunity Commission. (2021, December 1). *MedicOne Medical Response to pay $450,000 to resolve sexual harassment and retaliation lawsuit*. https://www.jdsupra.com/legalnews/medicone-medical-response-to-pay-450-5635510.

"Our diversity, equity, and inclusion efforts start with understanding the systemic bias and exclusion that exist in everyday life and their ripple effects on individual organizations and the world."[5] Importantly, learning about bias alone can be problematic. Work by Michelle Duguid and Melissa Thomas-Hunt has revealed that simply learning about bias can paradoxically create more bias because people support norms of stereotyping.[6] Hence, a critical second step is to move beyond just becoming aware of the bias and additionally be motivated to act. Instead of legitimizing bias, we want to reinforce a belief that people are trying to conquer their biases and you should, too. Or, as Adam Grant and Sheryl Sandberg state, we want to send a more effective message: "Most people don't want to discriminate, and you shouldn't either."[7] To do this requires action—you have to be motivated to make that change for yourself and for your organization. The third step is to make the necessary changes—to act. If not you, then whom? For every individual strategy that we discuss, the necessity of these three overarching steps is present. We now consider in some detail these individual-level strategies that targets of discrimination can adopt or actions that targets can take to reduce the bias that is directed at them.

Before we talk about these strategies, we emphasize that it is problematic to lay the burden of remediating bias on the shoulders of the targets themselves. However, there are many stigmatized people who ask, What can *we* do? What strategies should we adopt? How can we reduce the bias? There are a number of answers that can empower targets and strategies that show promise for altering discrimination.

---

[5] Yuan, E. (2022). *A letter from our CEO: Inaugural DEI report*. Retrieved from https://blog.zoom.us/zoom-dei-inaugural-report.

[6] Duguid, M. M., & Thomas-Hunt, M. C. (2015). Condoning stereotyping? How awareness of stereotyping prevalence impacts expression of stereotypes. *Journal of Applied Psychology, 100*(2), 343–359.

[7] Grant, A., & Sandberg, S. (2014, December 6). When talking about bias backfires. *The New York Times*. https://www.nytimes.com/2014/12/07/opinion/sunday/adam-grant-and-sheryl-sandberg-on-discrimination-at-work.html.

Passing or Covering

One option that some people take is to pass or to cover or hide the part of themselves that puts them at risk of facing discrimination. Aspects of identity such as neurodivergence, sexual orientation, or religion are not immediately visible to others and thus can be concealed. (Of course, many aspects of identity, such as race, age, and gender, tend to be more visible and are much more difficult to cover.) People with concealable characteristics make decisions about whether, to whom, how, and when to reveal or conceal that part of themselves that may be targeted by bias.

It has been reported that 61% of employees cover some aspect of themselves at work. Of these individuals, 29% said they changed their appearance (e.g., socioeconomic status and religion), 40% said they actively avoided or forestalled mentioning some affiliation (e.g., age and sexual orientation), 57% said they avoided sticking up for their in-group (e.g., race and gender), and 18% said that they avoided other members of their in-group (e.g., those with cancer or mental health issues).[8] One MBA student described their experience passing as straight by writing,

> As a gay person, I found myself always "passing" by carefully monitoring what I was saying to not out myself. I wouldn't talk much about my personal life and I tried my best to be as "masculine" as I could be. I have some privilege in that I'm somewhat masculine naturally, so it wasn't as much of an issue as [it would have been were I] more feminine, but it was exhausting to have to think about how everything I might say might be perceived.

Another MBA student described their experience with racial passing by stating,

> I am always, always, always assumed to be white. I am hesitant to correct this assumption because I have a deep-seated fear that people will think

---

[8] Yoshino, K., & Smith, C. (2014, March). Fear of being different stifles talent. *Harvard Business Review*.

I'm just looking for attention or trying to seem special by claiming my Latinx roots.

Passing or covering can protect people from being directly targeted by discrimination; if decision-makers believe a person to be White or straight, then that person may avoid some biases. However, it is important to recognize that hiding an important part of who you are can also be costly. In fact, research suggests that disclosing important identities can have a positive impact on psychological well-being and job experiences.

Acknowledging

An alternative to passing is acknowledgment, where people from marginalized backgrounds explicitly mention the aspect of their identity that is devalued. This kind of strategy can be useful because targets of bias often feel like everyone's looking at them or waiting for them to explain their situation. In American society, social norms suggest that it is impolite to ask about personal matters, so instead, it is expected that people might choose to reveal relevant information about themselves. Imagine, for instance, interacting with the person shown in Figure 9.1. He could use an acknowledgment strategy to reduce bias by simply stating, "As you see, I have a scar on my face." He could also choose to elaborate on the how or the why by further saying, "A dog bit me" or "It's from a car accident." Researchers have long proposed that acknowledgments are helpful because they can reduce uncertainty and anxiety. People might be worried about staring at the scar, or they may be preoccupied with questions about what caused the scar. Acknowledgment can reduce attention to a stigma and help people get beyond it.

We used an eye-tracking machine to explore how people's attention to a stigma changes after its acknowledgment.[9] The values on the

---

[9] Madera, J. M., & Hebl, M. (2019). To look or not to look: Acknowledging facial stigmas in the interview to reduce discrimination. *Personnel Assessment and Decisions*, 5(2), Article 3. https://doi.org/10.25035/pad.2019.02.003.

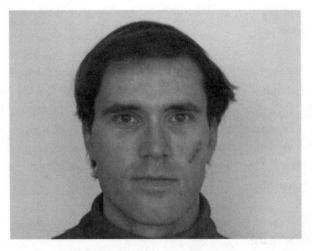

Figure 9.1 Participant in Madera and Hebl's (2019) study.

x-axis of Figure 9.2 represent the amount of time spent looking at the region of the face where there is a scar. The line at the bottom of the graph shows how much attention there is to the region when there is no stigma—this is the control or baseline attention. The other two lines show what happens when there is an acknowledgment (dashed line) versus no acknowledgment (black line). If there is an acknowledgment, there is attention to the scar region at first, but it decreases over time. Without the acknowledgment, people tend to look at the stigma. We look at it, and then we realize we shouldn't be looking at it, so we look away. And then we look at it again. And we think again, "No, we shouldn't be looking at it." And then we look again. So what the acknowledgment does is help reduce attention to the scar by letting us focus on it and then get over it.

Disclosing

A similar strategy that people can enact is to disclose their identity. Whereas acknowledging often involves describing a visible characteristic, disclosure involves addressing a part of identity that can be

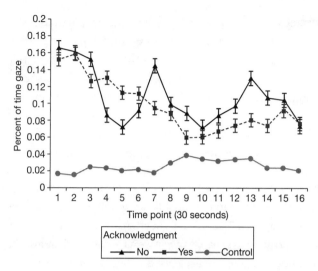

Figure 9.2 Stigma acknowledgment across time of an interview.

hidden. A gay co-worker might disclose their sexual orientation by saying, for example, "You may not have realized this, but I have a same-sex partner." The benefits of disclosure are many. For instance, being open about an important part of yourself can reduce stress, improve confidence, and enhance interpersonal relationships. Disclosure can also have indirect benefits for other colleagues by providing social support and by potentially mobilizing organizational support. It can also inspire organizations to adopt policies that protect and promote diversity. Disclosure can meaningfully shape social norms by helping create and enhance a culture of acceptance.

However—and it's a major however—disclosure has the potential to backfire. Disclosing a part of yourself also makes you vulnerable to a variety of negative reactions. Many people with concealable identities weigh the risks and benefits of these decisions very carefully.

Individuating

Another strategy that individuals can use is to individuate. Individuating means distinguishing yourself as a unique person.

This strategy can help people think beyond any particular stereotype to realize that a person is not just one thing. So, if a person wearing a hijab and an abaya describes something about herself that is not about her religion (e.g., that she is from Texas or likes soccer or has three dogs), we might stop thinking about her as being a Muslim woman. Instead, we will see her as an individual person who is not any one thing and is multidimensional. One of our female MBA students explained her need for and use of this strategy:

> As a well-site geologist I got to travel to a lot of places and usually when I pull up to a work location, most folks are unwilling to remotely help me figure out anything. This is usually not the case for my white colleagues. However, that always changes when we have our first daily meeting and I introduce myself as the geologist and boom, every junior staff fixes their act and are super nice to me.

Our research has shown that this kind of strategy can indeed reduce discrimination because it shifts attention away from narrow stereotypes.[10]

Reducing Justifications for Others' Discrimination

Most people want to see themselves as egalitarian, so they try to suppress their stereotypes and prejudice. But stereotypes and prejudice still result in discrimination because people come up with excuses or justifications for their negative views. We may generally try to hold back stereotypes about women because we know it is not socially acceptable, but when a female leader expresses emotion, our reaction might be "See, I told you women are too emotional to be leaders."

---

[10] King, E. B., & Ahmad, A. S. (2010). An experimental field study of interpersonal discrimination toward Muslim job applicants. *Personnel Psychology*, *63*(4), 881–906. https://doi.org/10.1111/j.1744-6570.2010.01199.x.

Given this, one approach for reducing discrimination is to eliminate the excuses or justifications that allow it to emerge. Consider a person who is heavy. There are a number of stereotypes associated with obesity that might lead to discrimination. A justification that often excuses discrimination toward heavy people is the belief that their condition is their own fault or that they are to blame. Our research found that when people who appear to be obese (by wearing obesity prosthetics or "fat" suits) said that they were on a diet and training for a half marathon, they encountered less discrimination than when they said they were not dieting or exercising. This suggests that reducing or addressing the excuses people have for discrimination can improve experiences.

Debunking Others' Stereotypes

Targets of discrimination can also debunk stereotypes. Employees with disabilities might explicitly address a stereotype that they are not flexible by directly conveying that they love to travel. Pregnant workers might state that they will not need any extra accommodation. What these direct statements sometimes do is bring the biases of others directly to the surface. They allow stereotypic expectations to be introduced as a problem and then immediately solved.

Compensating

Targets of discrimination who anticipate that they might receive negative treatment might also engage in compensatory behaviors or intentionally act in a way that draws favorable reactions. For instance, if we think someone does not like us, we might smile widely, be extra friendly, and give lots of compliments. The effectiveness of compensatory behaviors in reducing discrimination has been shown in several research studies. In one, researchers manipulated videos to show the expressions of Black and White store clerks while ringing up sales in a home goods shop.[11] The clerks either acted in a neutral but polite way or were smiling, warm, and friendly. In all videos, the sales clerks were equally efficient and knowledgeable. When viewers saw the employees performing fewer compensatory behaviors— when they behaved politely and efficiently—Black store clerks were rated as less friendly and as poorer performers than White clerks. In contrast, viewers of sales clerks who engaged in compensatory behaviors by acting extra friendly and positive rated the Black and White clerks similarly. So, in short, just being polite was not enough for the Black employees. Putting on a big smile was necessary to get the same performance ratings as the White employees. This confirms that compensatory behaviors can reduce discrimination, but it also highlights the potential costs of asking people from marginalized backgrounds to engage in this extra, burdensome labor.

Confronting

A very common strategy that targets can adopt is to confront discrimination. This involves directly addressing a prejudiced statement or discriminatory behavior that an offending individual has made. Imagine a gay employee who hears a colleague make a joke about gay people. The gay employee might say something very straightforward such as "Actually, I'm gay and the comment you made hurt my feelings." Likewise, imagine a Hispanic woman who hears a co-worker say that he would never hire Hispanic people for the job. She might respond by saying, "Michael, I've never thought of you as being the type of person who discriminates against Hispanic people. Can you explain that to me?" Confrontations, if done in ways that do not alienate people, can disrupt people's behaviors and get them to think more carefully about the actions they are adopting.

---

[11] Grandey, A. A., Houston, L., III, & Avery, D. R. (2019). Fake it to make it? Emotional labor reduces the racial disparity in service performance judgments. *Journal of Management, 45*(5), 2163–2192. https://doi.org/10.1177/0149206318757019.

A total of 48 of the 54 MBAs indicated that they had confronted prejudice and discrimination at least once in the workplace. We highlight a few of the responses they gave when they were asked how they specifically confronted bias in the workplace. Reflecting a number of individuals' strategies, one MBA student said, "I repeat their statement more slowly and question if that is what they actually mean." Another student described a two-step process of confrontation. She wrote,

> The key to confronting someone about being biased or discriminatory towards you is to be comfortable having the conversation and not let your emotions show too much (especially as a woman.) Step 1 [is to] acknowledge to the person what you have experienced from them or what you witnessed them say or do to someone else. Step 2 [is to] ask for clarity or if they understand why and then end it with some type of lesson or example relating it to them personally.

This kind of thoughtful, deliberate response may indeed be helpful in addressing discrimination.

Importantly, a confrontation strategy (like the other strategies described previously) is often cognitively and emotionally demanding. One female student stated, "I've thought that I should, but I'm always scared to." A Hispanic student said, "No, unfortunately, I have not confronted others about discriminatory behavior. I typically keep feelings like this to myself." An Asian woman stated she did not confront because she "was afraid of the ramifications." Finally, a Black man stated, "I have often been faced with subtle bias which is hard to prove. Especially since a lot of decisions are made in my absence and I do not know who is saying what about me."

Remembering

Mary Church Terrell, a Tennessee suffragist whose parents were born into slavery, helped start the National Association of Colored Women (NACW). She wrote,

And so, lifting as we climb, onward and upward we go, struggling and striving, and hoping that the buds and blossoms of our desires will burst into glorious fruition 'ere long. . . . Seeking no favors because of our color, nor patronage because of our needs, we knock at the bar of justice, asking for an equal chance.

The phrase "lifting as we climb" became the motto of the NACW, as Terrell pleaded with White suffragists to "stand up not only for the oppressed [women], but also for the oppressed race!" Targets of discrimination can indeed lift as they climb, supporting other targets and remembering the barriers they face while they work to ensure that those who come behind them find a better world.

Conclusion

In describing the strategies in this chapter, we reiterate that there are clearly some very major downsides to target-focused interventions. In *Whistling Vivaldi*, Claude Steele describes how his friend, Brent Staples, an African American journalist at *The New York Times*, strategically debunked stereotypes.[12] When Brent was a graduate student walking around what used to be a predominantly White neighborhood (Hyde Park in Chicago), he realized he was creating distress for the people he passed. He stated that people would get closer together or show other signs that they felt scared of his presence. To act against the stereotype, Brent decided to adopt the strategy of whistling Vivaldi's "Four Season" or some Beatles tunes when he was walking by White couples. Although this allowed Brent to reduce a stereotype of himself as a violent Black man and reduce the fear that others might have in passing by him, he also stated that it resulted in him feeling that he was pressured into having to adopt another group's culture or reality. This pressure, which researchers

---

[12] Steele, C., & Conan, N. (2010, April 12). *"Whistling Vivaldi" and beating stereotypes*. NPR. https://www.npr.org/templates/story/story.php?storyId=125859207.

have come to identify as a stereotype threat, creates stress and an inability to feel positive about one's own group and oneself.

Given that whistling Vivaldi and the other general strategies that we have discussed in this chapter place the burden on targets, it is important to consider strategies that do not further jeopardize targets who already experience victimization. Target strategies can be problematic if they offer only a fix-your-own-problem mentality. It is emotionally taxing to have this burden. Furthermore, people from minoritized backgrounds are often penalized for promoting diversity. So the answer is not to just rely on targets themselves—the need for others to help reduce bias is critical.

Tools for Working Together

1. Consider the biases that you or someone you care about are experiencing at work. How are you or your loved one dealing with them at present? What would be ideal? What are the advantages and disadvantages of acting how you would ideally like to act? What is standing in your way?
2. Face the experience by directly naming it and acknowledging feelings. Consider sharing this with the perpetrator. If this is too threatening and/or you fear retaliation, share the experience with a family member, friend, co-worker, or counselor.
3. Understand your and your loved ones' rights. Many of these can be found at https://www.eeoc.gov/youth/your-rights. Learn the steps that one needs to take when reporting discrimination within one's organization.
4. Consider keeping a journal to document not only the discriminatory behavior but also your feelings about the transgressions. Ignoring discrimination can often be unhealthy. Name it and use journaling to try to make sense of strategies that can be used to eliminate it and to healthily interpret the problem and your reactions.
5. Consider the strategies that you have read about in this chapter. Which ones do you think might be most and least effective?

10
What Can Allies Do?

Most employees in the workforce are straight. Plain and simple. Yet, many of these straight allies choose to play a role in reducing discrimination toward their LGBTQ+ co-workers. The difference that they can make is life-changing. In June 2016, a terrorist killed 49 people at Pulse, a gay nightclub in Florida. One of our MBA students recalls her army officer (a White, cis, straight, male) bringing in the entire brigade of more than 1,000 soldiers to address what happened. She remembers him saying,

> I want every single LGBTQ Soldier to know we have your back. If you're going to wear this uniform and represent my Army, you will respect every person to your left and right, despite your differences. We have zero tolerance for hate in our ranks and I would ask you to open your mind and hearts up a little to mourn with the LGBTQ community.

Our MBA student (also a member of the LGBTQ+ community) found this to be extremely impactful. This leader chose to be an ally when she and the LGBTQ+ community needed it most.

A blog on the popular gay traveler website, Nomadic Boys, highlights some of the greatest LGBTQ+ allies of all-time.[1] We draw attention to the top three and a few of the things they have done that have been deemed so effective to the LGBTQ+ community. The site lists Cher as number one on the list because she "has blasted [politicians] on Twitter for anti-equality policies, has turned down

---

[1] Arestis S. (2021, June 1). *20 best gay allies of all time.* https://nomadicboys.com/best-gay-allies.

an invitation to sing at the Russia Winter Olympics due to their anti-gay laws, and openly supported her son, Chaz Bono, through his transition." Indeed, these are not just statements but, rather, consistent actions that reflect her commitment to equality, which also includes befriending LGBT individuals in the 1970s; portraying a lesbian woman in 1983; and serving as a keynote speaker for the national Parents, Family, and Friends of Lesbians and Gays (PFFLG) convention.

Coming in at number two is the late Ruth Bader Ginsburg. The site praises Bader Ginsburg for voting to strike down Colorado's 1996 anti-gay amendment, to strike down Texas's 2003 law that criminalized sodomy, to support California's 2013 efforts toward equal marriage, and to support the *Obergefell v. Hodges* ruling that enabled full marriage equality in all 50 U.S. states. Bader Ginsburg did not use her celebrity platform (although her actions and dissenting opinions certainly grew her celebrity stature); rather, she dedicated herself and her work life to rewriting wrongs toward many marginalized individuals.

Few would anticipate that a Christian, country–western singer, whose popularity in large part comes from a conservative fan base, would be third on the list, but that is exactly where the Nomadic Boys place Dolly Parton. Not only did she sing progressive gay-friendly lyrics back in 1991 and record an Academy Award–nominated song for a story about a trans woman's journey but also she supports drag humorously, saying that "some of them look more like me than I do," and makes very clear her beliefs that LGBTQ individuals are often oppressed by conservatives.[2] When she learned that a lady at the Dollywood Splash Country amusement park was forced to turn her "Marriage is so Gay" T-shirt inside-out, Parton publicly stated,

---

[2] Broverman, N. (2018, December 7). 8 times Dolly Parton cemented her status as an LGBTQ icon. *Advocate*. https://www.advocate.com/music/2018/12/07/8-times-dolly-parton-cemented-her-status-lgbtq-icon#media-gallery-media-1.

I am truly sorry for the hurt or embarrassment regarding the gay and lesbian T-shirt incident at Dollywood's Splash Country. Everyone knows of my personal support of the gay and lesbian community. Dollywood is a family park and all families are welcome.[3]

In defining a lesbian couple as a family, Parton showed that she was not afraid to take a stand, despite the fact that it was possible she might risk boycotts of her parks and brands and damage to her reputation. Instead, Parton sings on, just as she has done most recently with Miley Cyrus, singing "Rainbowland," where "we're free to be exactly who we are"—a song that was axed from an elementary school program because it was deemed inappropriate.[4]

What these three allies show is that there are a variety of actions that allies can take to be effective, and this same truth extends to allies in the workplace. Such employees may be allies to LGBTQ co-workers and/or they may be allies to any number of other marginalized co-workers. A study by Working Mother Research Institute[5] asked women how their male co-workers can be effective allies for them, and the most common responses that women gave included the following: 83% of women said that male allies should address inappropriate behavior and attitudes of others, 82% said that allies should acknowledge that racism can exist in the workplace, 81% said that they should not interrupt or talk over women in meetings, and 81% said that they should better understand the barriers that women face. In this chapter, we describe and unpack ally behaviors that may be most effective in the workplace.

---

[3] Bledsoe, W. (2011, August 2). *Dolly Parton responds to Dollywood Splash Country T-shirt controversy.* https://archive.knoxnews.com/news/local/dolly-parton-responds-to-dollywood-splash-country-t-shirt-controversy-ep-403504862-357637141.html.

[4] Laub, A. (2023, March 28). *Wisconsin school axes first-graders' performance of "Rainbowland" by Miley Cyrus and Dolly Parton.* CBS News. https://www.cbsnews.com/news/miley-cyrus-and-dolly-parton-rainbowland-song-performed-first-graders-axed-wisconsin-school.

[5] Bowers, Katherine. "Men as Allies." Working Mother, 17 February 2016, www.workingmother.com/men-as-allies

Educate Oneself and Become Aware

Allyship must begin with awareness—it is impossible to help when you don't even realize there is a problem. That means getting outside of yourself, listening, and learning. Mikki was in college when a racist incident happened to a Black female student (i.e., an object reflecting racial hatred was left outside her dormitory room). The Black Student Association announced that it would be holding a rally on campus and invited everyone to attend to show support for the victim as well as more general support for Black students on campus. Many people attended the rally, and the organizers spontaneously decided that they would have the procession march through campus. At first, it was unclear who should walk in the march, but the Black Student Association organizers thought that the Black women should walk alone. The non-Black women wanted to walk, too, to show their support, and some Black women agreed. But many of the allies felt uncertain about what they should do: Should they remain in place or follow their intuition and march along? How should they best signify their support? It wasn't entirely clear what the allies should have done—something many allies experience across a number of different contexts. And, of course, the discomfort that the allies were feeling was nothing compared to what many of the Black women were feeling and/or had felt. What the allies needed to do was purposely decenter themselves and sit with and learn from the discomfort they were feeling. It was about watching and taking their lead from those who were suffering. It was about becoming aware. And those who were suffering wanted to walk alone.

Part of being an ally is realizing that it's not about meeting one's own needs—it's about meeting someone else's needs. And that often involves realizing that one is privileged, an insight that often leads people to feel guilty and/or try to justify oneself. But sometimes the most important thing to do is to identify and sit with the anxiety and then refocus one's attention on other people. It's about listening and learning about what other people want and need. In the case of the march, it was about understanding that Black student organizers and many of the Black women marching wanted and needed to stand together, alone. And it was about the allies being present to support their voices and decisions.

Allies can offer a tremendous amount of social support by generally being aware, listening, encouraging, and supporting coworkers who face biases in the workplace. The power of allyship can be tremendous. Allies can provide protection against loneliness and feelings of isolation. One of our MBA students stated, "I also have found comfort in talking to my other Asian and female peers about my experiences. Sometimes I just feel better after ranting." Allies become aware by lending an ear, but allyship does not stop at passively listening to targets of discrimination.

Fight Conformity

It is difficult for people to behave in ways that are counternormative. People desperately want to fit in and to belong, so they typically go along to get along—they conform. This makes some allyship behaviors incredibly difficult to enact. You are probably reading this right now thinking, "Oh, I know other people are scared, but if I saw discrimination I would definitely call it out." We hope that is true, but the data suggest that it is not. Most people will go along with whatever everyone else is doing.

A powerful social psychology experiment from the 1950s, which has been replicated in many forms throughout the decades, demonstrates this tendency to conform.[6] The researchers brought a number of participants into the lab and asked them to sit at a table. As shown in the configuration in Figure 10.1, some of the participants were fake (they were actors trained to behave a certain way) and one was real. An experimenter told participants they would be making judgments about objects. The researchers were interested in how the single "real" participant would respond to a situation in which they had to fight against the pressure to conform.

---

[6] Asch, S. E. (1956). Studies of independence and conformity: I. A minority of one against a unanimous majority. *Psychological Monographs: General and Applied, 70*(9), 1–70.

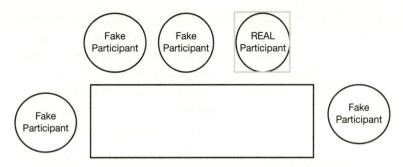

Figure 10.1 Configuration of participants in Asch's (1956) study.

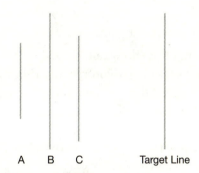

Figure 10.2 Example of lines from Asch's (1956) study.

The participants were asked to make a judgment for which there was an obvious and factually correct answer. Participants were presented with three separate lines, as shown in Figure 10.2, and were asked to make an obvious choice about which of three lines (A, B, or C) matched the target line. The answer is B (no illusions here!). The experimenters wanted to know whether the "real" participant would go along with the wrong answer if everyone else did.

The data were very convincing. If all the fake participants said the longest line was A, so did the real participant. Nearly every person, nearly every time. Why? No one wants to be the one to be different. No one wants to be the one to stand up and risk facing scrutiny, retaliation, or ridicule. If everyone else is doing something and they are not, they start to think that maybe they are the ones who are wrong.

People want to fit in, to be liked, to belong, so they will go along with an answer they believe to be wrong just to be like everyone else.

But this series of studies also addressed a very important second question: What does it take to get the real participant to break conformity? When will people stand up for what they know is right? In the line judgment task, it took just one other person. When one fake participant went against the grain and said that B was the right answer, the real participant did too. It only took one person, one voice, one action to make a difference.

Act

One of the most important things allies can do after educating themselves and becoming aware is to confront discrimination. One of our MBA students indicated the positive effect of her supportive behavior toward another woman. She stated,

> [I] had a male coworker that would consistently speak over women. I noticed he would tone it down when called out on it but most women never spoke up about it. Towards the end of my time at that company I began using this line, "Stephanie, I think you were hitting on an important point before you were interrupted, can we revisit?" The interruptions slowed down dramatically.

This illustrates a behavioral response that goes beyond awareness.

In fact, evidence suggests that it is more effective for individuals who are not personally targeted by discrimination to confront it. This is one of the key takeaways that we got from reading Dolly Chugh's poignant book *The Person You Mean to Be*.[7] In it, she articulates that if you are a majority group member, you have ordinary privilege of which you may not even be aware. But because of this privilege, your voice is heard differently. And so, if you overhear or witness discrimination against a minority group, you must realize that it is your

---

[7] Chugh, D. (2018). *The person you mean to be: How good people fight bias*. HarperCollins.

place to speak up. Indeed, targets' concerns are often minimized as personal complaints, whereas majority group members are seen as more accurate observers. In addition, allies who are not themselves from a marginalized group have more power to influence others. Perhaps not surprisingly, men are more supportive of gender equity initiatives that are pitched by other men than when they originate with women. In a study we conducted,[8] men read an article that focused on gender equity. In some conditions, the article was authored by a man, whereas in others, it was authored by a woman. Men were much more supportive of gender equity after reading an article they thought was written by a man rather than a woman. If that's not enough motivation to involve men as allies, evidence also suggests that whereas marginalized group members sometimes face social penalties when they advocate for diversity, equity, and inclusion (DEI), White men who advocate on behalf of White women and people of color are in fact rewarded for these actions with higher performance ratings![9]

So what should allies do? General advice would be to ensure that you recruit, promote, and raise the visibility of people from marginalized backgrounds. Box 10.1, provides some of the specific behaviors that our MBA students have experienced in their careers. In addition to these general recommendations, we also believe it would be helpful to ask any targeted group about the issues that they specifically experience as helpful or unhelpful in any particular situation.[10] When in doubt, ask people what they think would be helpful or how they would like to be supported.

But not every act of confrontation is an effective one. For instance, a significant percentage of our female MBA students indicated that they had commonly experienced male co-workers who were allies

---

[8] Hebl, M. R., Corrington, A., Fa Kaji, N., Trump-Steele, R. C. E., & Nittrouer, C. L. (2022). *Engaging feMANists: How to get men to support women's issues* [Unpublished manuscript]. Rice University.

[9] Hekman, D. R., Johnson, S. K., Foo, M. D., & Yang, W. (2017). Does diversity-valuing behavior result in diminished performance ratings for non-White and female leaders? *Academy of Management Journal, 60*(2), 771–797.

[10] Cheng, S., Ng, L., Traylor, A., & King, E. B. (2019). Helping or hurting? Understanding women's perceptions of male allies. *Personnel Assessment Decisions, 5*, 44–54.

> **Box 10.1 Effective Ally Behaviors, as Reported by MBA Students**
>
> - Inviting me to showcase my work and get a larger group of senior workers to recognize me and my contributions.
> - Immediately shutting down negative conversation and pivoting back to actual work.
> - Reporting the bias—calling managers and HR.
> - Validating me.
> - Confronting someone about what they said to me, saying it was not right and discriminatory.
> - Making me feel safe and seen.
> - Encouraging me and providing me with instrumental support.
> - Giving me advice.
> - Helping me believe in myself.
> - Connecting me with people and sharing knowledge and experience.
> - Vouching for me.
> - Valuing me and my contributions and made it evident to all who would listen.
> - Extending his network to me.
> - Providing a safe space for me.
> - Providing a stellar recommendation.
> - Fighting for a higher salary for me.
> - Making me feel comfortable being myself.
> - Giving me the credit in front of senior management.
> - Stressing my contributions to leadership.
> - Including me in crucial meetings.
> - Always backing me up.
> - Anticipating what I need in the situation to feel safe.
> - Ask what I need in a challenging time.
> - Assisting me in elevating my concerns.

in private but did not walk the walk that they talked in public. In one example, a woman who was appointed to lead a project faced anger from a male colleague who thought he deserved the position. When the woman consulted with another male co-worker on the team to see if he could help her during meetings (e.g., keep the upset man from dominating and end unproductive rants), the male ally said he would help. However, this never came to fruition in any of the meetings. The male ally was privately supportive of the female-appointed leader but did not help when others were around. In addition to this important theme of consistency in allyship across public and private settings, our students also noted a number of other ineffective behaviors, which are listed in Box 10.2.

Assume Psychological Standing and Use It

A few years ago, Emma Watson gave a talk at the United Nations headquarters for the HeforShe Campaign inviting men to support women. It seemed odd that they would need an invitation, but as Watson stated, "How can we affect change in the world when only half of it is invited or feel welcome to participate in the conversation?" More than 2.25 million men worldwide signed the global commitment to gender equality.[11] What Watson was doing was trying to give *psychological standing* to men, or convey that men had a stake in the matter, that their voices were important, and that they needed to be heard.

This is important because often dominant group members (e.g., men and White people) do not feel like it is their place to speak up, particularly when it is in a sphere in which women or minorities are present for them to say something themselves. We have found that most people can tell when subtle bias is happening—people know when something isn't quite right—but, unfortunately, most people from dominant groups don't feel responsible for responding to subtle bias. Apparently, if the issues are about White women or

[11] https://www.heforshe.org/en.

Box 10.2 Ineffective Ally Behaviors

- Talking the talk but not walking the walk.
- No regular or consistent mentoring.
- Not taking a public stand.
- Standing silent while racist comments and jokes are made.
- Any version of mansplaining to "help me understand."
- Giving me bad advice.
- Not caring or even pretending to.
- Window dressing.
- Reaching out to me for educational resources instead of finding them himself.
- Not listening.
- Not being given a deserved promotion.
- Downplaying my needs.
- Being unable to consider my own individual needs.
- Overlooking me for a bonus.
- Being told to cover or remain inauthentic.
- Seeing allies abandon you when they have skin in the game.
- Interrupting me in meetings.
- Sexually harassing me.
- Not being taken seriously or responded to when reporting company violations.
- Physically avoiding me.
- Not responding to complaints.
- Discouraging me from wanting to succeed.
- Saying unsavory comments to me.
- Not supporting me when others harassed me.
- Cutting me off during meetings.
- Not allowing my voice to be heard.
- Harassing me.
- Ignoring me.
- Not responding to employee complaints.
- Not taking stressful situations involving diverse employees seriously.

about people of color, many men and White people believe that they should just let the women and people of color respond. Members of the dominant group reported not being sure what to do, being perceived as trying to take over, or as "man/race-splaining." What needs to happen instead is that men (or allies in general) need to feel psychological standing. Psychological standing is a sense of legitimacy to perform an action with respect to a cause—feeling like it is legitimate for you to speak up or do something when the situation demands.

A helpful article describes the imperative for men and other dominant group members to get involved with gender parity initiatives.[12] They report feeling like "it's not my place to say anything about [Black people, women, etc.] because I haven't experienced what they've experienced" or "I'm not [Black, female, etc.], so I shouldn't say anything—I should just listen." As we have already mentioned, it is important to listen, but it is critical to also speak up. Speaking up is a way of signaling that allies stand with, are listening, and are supporting targets. And when targets have allies, targets have much more power. So allies can in fact empower targets by getting involved.

An example from one of our MBA students shows exactly how this can happen. When asked to explain effective allyship, she described her favorite colleague. He was someone that all the other male colleagues really liked, respected, and wanted to emulate. In one meeting, some of her male colleagues were saying that her solution to a structural engineering issue would never work, and they wouldn't let her speak. As she described, "My friend handed me an Expo marker and told me to just start writing on our office white board. Eventually the others stopped talking and started following my calculations on the wall." After this, they were able to have a constructive dialogue and understand her proposed solution. Similarly, another female MBA reflected on a meeting she had led in which some co-workers were openly questioning her ability to lead

---

[12] Sherf, E. N., & Tangirala, S. (2017, September 13). How to get men involved with gender parity initiatives. *Harvard Business Review*.

the team given her lack of prior experience in the company. Upon hearing these dismissive comments, her senior manager stood up in the meeting and publicly emphasized his confidence in her abilities. After this, the engineers no longer made dismissive comments about her experience. Another female Black MBA student described a situation in which White male colleague called out another White male for his discriminatory behavior. She explained, "It was very nice to know I had white male allies who would speak up for me in spaces that I am not in."

Several other MBA students described similar experiences with race. One MBA student wrote that one of the most effective ally strategies he had experienced was "having a White friend defend me when racist jokes are made—it is much more effective than when I try to defend myself." Similarly, another Black MBA student indicated the allyship of a White man by stating, "When someone says or does something that we perceive as discriminatory, he always backs me up and is very good as anticipating what I need in the situation to feel safe." So how does one strike the balance between trying not to be the savior and standing up for targets of bias? We think the answer to this comes from learning what targets most want and do not want, and then acting accordingly.

Stand Up in the Absence of Targets Too

Allies must speak up in the presence of targets of bias, but they must also make allyship a consistent behavior, whether the target is present or absent. One of our MBA students recalled a situation in which a person made disparaging remarks about Latinx people and immigrants. While she spoke up, her ally remained silent. This eroded her trust in them as an ally because, in her words, "if they would not speak up for me when I was there, then they definitely would not speak up for me when I was not there." Allies can provide evidence that employees who are targets of bias are actually doing their jobs well, that they're effective workers, and that they don't deserve the unfair treatment that they're receiving regardless of their physical presence.

By learning, fighting conformity, and standing up in these ways, allies can make a huge impact on DEI.

Tools for Working Together

Consider the acronym ALLIES: Access and opportunities, Listen and Learn, Include and collaboration, Encourage balance, and Share (Figure 10.3). As you learn more about each idea, consider the extent to which you engage in allyship behaviors directed toward marginalized individuals in your workplace or life.

For A, focus on marginalized colleagues and write down specific examples of when you have asked them for their input, asked about their accomplishments, amplified others' ideas and achievements, interrupted interrupters, and/or nominated others for awards. These behaviors help your colleagues be seen and heard.

For LL, write down some examples of when you have specifically noticed the racial/gender makeup (be it of collaborators, panelists, committee, or leaders), focused on educating yourself

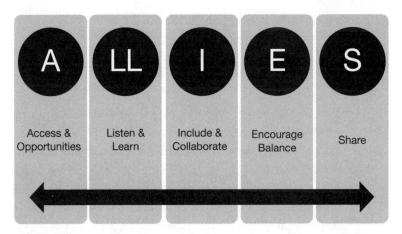

Figure 10.3 ALLIES acronym.

about the experiences of marginalized individuals, attended diversity training and other-related events, asked marginalized others about their experiences, and just listened. These behaviors prevent your marginalized colleagues from being overtaxed with educating others.

For I, write down some examples of times when you have collaborated with marginalized others, attended their presentations, mentored or sponsored them, shared information with them, invited them to social outings, and/or presented them with honest feedback. These behaviors offer inclusion and collaborative opportunities for marginalized colleagues.

For E, write down times when you have encouraged marginalized others to maintain balance. Perhaps you have been mindful of formal activity times, known and used family-friendly policies, and/or let women decide if they are/are not too busy. These behaviors help shoulder domestic demands, prevent penalties for using policies when men do not, and prevent women from being "protected" from challenging work.

For S, write down times when you have shared with your colleagues the value of diversity, challenges to equal opportunities, and your commitment to diversity. Describe if/when you possibly volunteered for committees with the purpose of being an ally/advocate for diversity.

If your page looks rather blank (and even if it does not), consider changing the questions from "How have you . . . ?" to "How might you in the future . . . ?"

***

Consider getting a group of allies and targets together to brainstorm ways that you can help targets who are in need. We did this in our own department after the George Floyd murder. We specifically came up with ways that we could help support Black colleagues. An abbreviated list of some of the things we generated is provided in Box 10.3. What problem might your group take on and what solutions might your group come up with? What are tangible things you can do?

***

Box 10.3 Examples of Ways Allies Can Support Black Colleagues

- Actively educate yourself (e.g., read *How to Be Anti-Racist* by Ibram Kendi).
- Don't lean on your Black friends to educate you.
- Realize your White privilege.
- Recognize and sit with any discomfort you are feeling—guilt and shame often accompany privilege.
- Spread the knowledge that you gain when you educate yourself.
- Check on the mental health of your African American friends.
- Be open to understanding.
- Actively listen to others—not to respond, but to understand.
- Understand the injustice—stand together.
- Support the Black community.
- Hold the people in your environment accountable for their unsupportive actions.
- Combat stereotypes.
- Recognize racist policies and work toward changing them.
- Protest.
- Avoid villainizing the protesters.
- Sign petitions for government actions.
- Call and email representatives and those who can make/enforce change.
- Donate toward supportive causes and candidates.
- Vote.

Consider forming or supporting a book club that encourages and supports learning about diverse perspectives and background, ideally that match some of the potentially marginalized employees in your workplace. This may be held over a lunch break, could happen virtually, or could be a weekend book-themed party. Encourage people who are and/or want to be allies to attend. Choosing books that focus on DEI in the workplace can help marginalized individuals feel supported and can help allies learn how to best display their support.

11
What Can Organizations Do?

At the height of the COVID-19 pandemic and when no vaccine was yet available, many people were afraid to leave their homes and return to working with others. This was particularly the case for some physically disabled individuals who were at heightened risk for serious illness from contracting COVID-19. For many organizations, the answer was obvious—make reasonable accommodations. But for other organizations, such as a Texas-based coffee company, it was not.[1] Rather, the coffee company denied employees' reasonable accommodation requests (e.g., to avoid working the drive-through window) and also stated that employees could not return to work until a vaccine was developed. Later, they were terminated. The U.S. Equal Employment Opportunity Commission found the company to be in violation of the Americans with Disabilities Act (ADA) and required that they provide financial relief to the affected employees, create and disseminate a policy that details the regulations applicable under the ADA and procedures to follow if/when future accommodations are requested, and provide annual training to managers and employees. Ideally, organizations are leading the change to be more inclusive and not being forced to do so by lawsuits.

Ironically, at another coffee shop called Bitty and Beau's Coffee, customers line up outside waiting to be served by many people who have disabilities.[2] The founder, Amy Wright, has two children with Down syndrome and decided she wanted to show (with federal or

---

[1] https://www.eeoc.gov/newsroom/151-coffee-pay-70000-settle-eeoc-disability-discrimination-lawsuit.

[2] Lerhfeld, J., & Gans, A. (2022, May 31). A human rights movement "disguised as a coffee shop" employs and empowers people with disabilities. *USA Today*. https://www.usatoday.com/story/money/2022/05/31/jobs-disability-discrimination-coffee-shop/9842243002.

state subsidies) that she could operate a prosperous business by employing people with disabilities. As one of Wright's coffee shop directors said, "It isn't hard to hire somebody with a disability. You just got to make tweaks and innovate around their needs."[3] What began as a one-shop coffee stop has successfully expanded to 17 locations throughout the United States, with one of its shops being 1 mile away from where we wrote this book.[4]

Sometimes we think of people with disabilities as not being able to do something because of their condition. However, this isn't true; rather, it's the environment that has not been truly set up to be inclusive of them. As one of our MBA students noted,

> There are adapted golf clubs for those who use a wheelchair. Imagine telling all people to use a bent golf club. They would struggle at the very things that allow those with disabilities to succeed. Everyone should be able to succeed.

Indeed, if we have never had one, it is hard to envision or understand the experiences of someone who has a physical disability. But organizations can and should adapt environments so more people have the opportunity to perform.

In this vein, it is important for organizations to reflect on the many ways that they can include others. In his article "Diversity as Strategy," David Thomas[5] presents a case analysis of IBM's decision to identify diversity as a strategic focus area. This strategic focus began from the notion of "constructive disruption," which invited radical change. The process involved the establishment of eight task forces, each led by well-respected executives and each representing a particular constituency group, with the goal of learning from

---

[3] Toner, K. (2017, December 17). How a cup of coffee becomes a "human rights movement." CNN. https://www.cnn.com/2017/06/22/health/cnnheroes-amy-wright-bitty-and-beaus-coffee/index.html.

[4] Sandler, E. (2023, January 16). *"Radically inclusive" new coffee shop empowers staff with disabilities in Rice Village.* CultureMap. https://houston.culturemap.com/news/restaurants-bars/radically-inclusive-new-coffee-shop-empowers-staff-with-disabilities-in-rice-village.

[5] Thomas, D. A. (2004, September). Diversity as strategy. *Harvard Business Review.* https://hbr.org/2004/09/diversity-as-strategy.

differences to improve business. After some resistance, conflict, dialogue, action, and time, the strategic organizational change process yielded a number of positive outcomes for diversity, equity, and inclusion (DEI) and for the business.

This strategic approach has been increasingly emphasized in the two decades since IBM's work. Indeed, a thoughtful and well-resourced approach to DEI that is integrated across every organization function should be based on a clear strategy. Organizations have the opportunity to begin to meet the realistic, economic, and moral imperatives of DEI through strategic choices and investments. One of the first ways that they should do this is by holistically identifying the specific problems and needs of their particular organization, which can be done by using an organizational needs analysis.

Organizational Needs Analysis

In an attempt to understand how health care organizations throughout the United States could better serve LGBT populations, researchers in 2018[6] surveyed 5,980 staff members and 638 leaders from 18 different health care organizations to examine deficits in practices, comfort, knowledge, and services. The important results of this analysis revealed that most clinicians rarely or never talked to their patients about their gender identity (72%) or sexual orientation (55%). They avoided these topics because they did not feel comfortable, did not want to offend their patients, did not have experience, did not know the proper language to use, or did not believe that it was necessarily related to care. This analysis—just one very basic type of needs analysis—importantly revealed deficits in the health care that LGBT individuals receive. If one's sexual orientation or gender identity is not known, how can the psychological and physical-related medical needs and issues associated with them be practiced?

---

[6] Goldhammer, H., Maston, E. D., Kissock, L. A., Davis, J. A., & Keuroghlian, A. S. (2018). National findings from an LGBT healthcare organizational needs assessment. *LGBT Health*, 5(8), 461–468.

A needs analysis is one of the most powerful tools that organizations can use to study, reflect upon, and optimize their workplaces. There are several different types of needs analyses that may have to do with a singular person, with a work group, or with an entire organization; and needs analysis may have to do with particular tasks, performance, content, training suitability, or a cost–benefit analysis. We focus on a type of needs analysis that is very germane to our understanding of the workplace—that of the organization as a whole.[7]

An organizational needs analysis is a formal process of systematically identifying weaknesses in, deficiencies of, or needs of an organization so that recruitment, training, and other actions can be deployed to enhance the success and desired outcomes of the organization. In short, it asks stakeholders to think about the organization's goals, the purpose, and the ideal operations and workforce versus what is actually happening. A needs analysis allows people to understand the gap between what is ideal and what is actually occurring.

If you do not periodically conduct a needs analysis, people and practices within an organization are often out of alignment. There can be complexities and conflict, and there is a lack of a link between purpose and design. People are engaging in behaviors or making trade-offs that are not relevant to the goals. So, the goals get completely ignored, behaviors get misaligned, and you sometimes end up further from your starting point. Therefore, you always need to be constantly asking, What problem are we trying to solve or what goal are we working toward? To begin, we suggest that you explicitly reflect on the purpose and objectives of the organization. You need to articulate the answers to questions such as What does the organization do? How does it function? and To what end? You might also ask or reflect on some of the questions listed in Box 11.1.

---

[7] Kuhnert, K. W., & Lahey, M. A. (2019). Approaches to organizational needs assessment. In R. Golembiewski (Ed.), *Handbook of organizational consultation* (pp. 830–841). Routledge.

> **Box 11.1 Reflection Questions About Your Organization as Part of a Needs Analysis**
>
> What do you want to change?
> What are the main issues: Climate? Turnover? Absenteeism? Accidents? Conflict? Sexual harassment? Resistance to change? Discrimination? Motivation? Productivity? Other difficulties?
> What outcome do you hope to see?
> How will you know if the outcome is successful?
> How will you know if the outcome is unsuccessful?
> How can you make the outcome most impactful?
> What do top management, middle management, entry-level workers want as outcomes?
> What current challenges are you facing?
> From your perspective, why does your company/organization need to make a change?
> What are the consequences if you do not make a change?
> What industry standards or evolving practices are impacting employees or might impact desired outcomes?
> How will you maintain success once it has initially been achieved?
> What resources will you need to galvanize to achieve change?

Goal Setting

Goal setting is a powerful tool to have when you are optimizing the workplace. The theory of goal setting[8] proposes that people make calculated decisions about their desired goals (particularly under certain conditions). Importantly, once individuals determine the goals that they want to achieve, they will use these goals to direct and motivate efforts to attain them. These goals work because they direct attention and action. They mobilize people's efforts and actions. At

---

[8] Locke, E. A., & Latham, G. P. (1990). *A theory of goal setting & task performance*. Prentice-Hall.

the organizational level, setting goals means setting a benchmark for progress. This can help ensure there is clarity and consensus around strategic priorities, thereby driving individual and unit behavior toward achieving those shared objectives.

The literature shows that goal setting is most likely to lead to desirable outcomes when the goals are SMART. To start, the goals should be specific (S) compared to being too vague or too large—the goals should be clearly communicated to and understood by stakeholders. To ensure goals are SMART, ask yourself, "Could it be more specific in terms of who will do what and how they will be held accountable?"

The goals also should be measurable (M), in that you can define progress toward them in some measurable way and that you can reevaluate this progress when necessary. To ensure goals are measurable, ask yourself, "How exactly will I measure that I have met my goals?"

The goals should be attainable (A), in that you should be able to accomplish them both by having the ability to do so and by being able to meet the goals within the allotted time. To ensure the goals are attainable, ask yourself, "Do I have the time, resources, and know-how to meet the goals?"

The goals should be relevant (R), meaning that they should align with organizational values and desired outcomes, particularly as specified in the organizational needs analysis. To ensure the goals are relevant, ask yourself, "Is the work that I am doing improving the likelihood that I will attain my organizational needs? Will I be closer to attaining them with my work?"

Finally, the goals should be time-based (T), in that they are realistic, ambitious, and include time-based breakdowns of activities to accomplish with the end date in site. To ensure that the goals are time-based, ask yourself, "Do I have a schedule? Do I know when certain things should be completed, with an overarching end goal date in sight, too?"

SMART goals are key to ensuring that your organization works toward fulfilling the its' strategic priorities. Once you have fully articulated the overarching outcomes and goals that are desired, the next step is to perform a SWOT analysis, which is a tool for analyzing your organization's strengths and weaknesses as well as the opportunities and threats it faces. Careful consideration of each of these factors[9] can help with the development of a strategy.

When completing the SWOT analysis, we focus first on the *now*. Thinking about strengths, or the characteristics that offer an advantage, can help organizations identify areas or resources that can be leveraged for change. Focusing next on weaknesses, or characteristics that place the organization at a disadvantage relative to others, can help direct development.

We then shift toward the *future*. We think about opportunities, or the elements in the environment that could be exploited to accomplish our goals. Opportunities may reflect areas for investment or effort. Finally, consideration of threats, which are elements in the environment that could provide setbacks to accomplishing the goals, ensures that appropriate flexibility is built into the change process.

In summary, the strengths are things that are good now. They can be maintained, expanded, and leveraged. Weaknesses are things that are bad now. We want to remedy and stop them. Opportunities can be prioritized and optimized. And we think of threats in the future that we want to avoid to ensure that our efforts are successful.

In conducting a SWOT analysis and developing strategic goals, we recommend keeping several key ideas in mind. These are necessary but insufficient features of any successful DEI strategy. They are discussed in the following section.

Top Management Buy-In and Participation

Diversity initiatives must be led, supported, believed, and championed by leaders at all levels of organizations. Peter Pisters, chief executive officer (CEO) of MD Anderson, is an example of this. When he arrived at MD Anderson in 2017, he asked, "What would it take for us to be number 1 in diversity?" And since then,

---

[9] Teoli, D., Sanvictores, T., & An, J. (2021). SWOT analysis. [Updated September 8, 2021]. In *StatPearls* [Internet]. StatPearls. https://www.ncbi.nlm.nih.gov/books/NBK537302.

he turned the dial. He has hired women and physicians from underrepresented ethnic backgrounds into key executive, leadership positions. He has empowered the diversity council and strengthened employee network groups for women, multicultural employees, LGBT+, employees who have cancer, disabled employees, and military veterans. He has enhanced transparency and connects with employees; he has given national keynote addresses on the power of diversity; he has helped facilitate discounts on day care; and he supports events such as "fusion of inclusion," in which employees host tables that showcase their heritage by proudly displaying attire, activities, lifestyles, food, and clothing. As he stated in 2021, "I want MD Anderson to be seen as an exemplar in our work on diversity, equity, and inclusion,"[10] and indeed it is.[11]

Leaders can address not only their own individual biases but also those embedded in their organizations. Leaders can set and execute policy, model and reinforce social norms, and empower human resources (HR) and other units to prioritize DEI. Leaders can ensure that employees see and believe that DEI is taken seriously in the organization. Our research has shown that people who are most resistant to supporting DEI also tend to be those who respect people in positions of authority; as a result, leaders with formal positions of authority may be the only ones who can positively impact people who otherwise resist DEI.[12]

We know of some DEI consultants who will politely but firmly decline engagements if the C-suite (i.e., executive managers) is not directly involved. When top-level leaders are not engaged in DEI directly, their followers learn that DEI is not an authentic priority for the organization. If a CEO attends a diversity training opportunity, it sends a clear message to employees that they too should

---

[10] Peter Pisters: I want MD Anderson to be seen as an exemplar in our work on diversity, equity, and inclusion. (2021, July 16). *The Cancer Letter*, *47*(28). https://cancerletter.com/health-equity/20210716_3.

[11] Advisory Board. (2022, April 29). The 90 best health care employers for diversity, according to *Forbes*. https://www.advisory.com/daily-briefing/2022/04/29/forbes-diversity.

[12] Lindsey, A., King, E. B., & Membere, A. (2017, July 28). Two types of diversity training that really work. *Harvard Business Review*. https://hbr.org/2017/07/two-types-of-diversity-training-that-really-work.

show up. Engagement from top-level leaders is a necessary but insufficient condition to creating and building inclusive organizational cultures.

DEI Initiatives That Transcend the Organization and Are Not Just Restricted to Human Resources

Every stakeholder should be aware of, engaged in, and accountable to DEI strategy. Often, organizations label diversity a management problem and house related disputes, resolutions, and management of it entirely within HR. It is easy to spot how progressive an organization is with its DEI initiatives by looking at the launching of diversity initiatives: Do they all come from HR, or are they integrated across units and functions? If DEI strategy is siloed in HR, it is too easily dismissed, overlooked, or ignored. An integrated, strategic approach to DEI means that every unit and person in an organization needs to be involved.

Organizational Messaging, Backed Up by Corporate Actions

In a *Harvard Business Review* article, 11 CEOs talked about what has worked in their organizations as they attempt to champion diversity. The most common things that they noted were to (a) lead by example when it comes to diversity, (b) hold themselves and others accountable on diversity initiatives, (c) foster diversity throughout the organization, and (d) broaden their perspectives on diversity and learning. In our research, we found that organizations which signaled support for anti-racist efforts with formal statements were rewarded with higher ratings of inclusion and, ultimately, greater profits. But our research has also shown that actions can speak louder than words—that organizational messages of support are most effective if they are accompanied by action. One of our MBA students described a powerful example of organizational messages that were backed up by meaningful actions:

> Two days after the Charlottesville Unite the Right gathering, I encountered a White Nationalist gathering on my way to work. I was extremely shaken from the event and told my work team I would not be in the office to meet my new manager. The new manager understood and scheduled multiple 1:1 meetings with me to figure out ways to support me. He made it clear that he, as a white male, could never fully understand the way I could have felt but wanted to do everything he could to support me. He ended up advocating for me to attend the National Black MBA conference. There, I was able to connect with many Black employees in and outside my company. My manager knew that I really wanted to go to the conference, and I was thankful that he did what he could to get me there. He also prompted me to schedule a meeting with a senior Black leader on the HR team who was a good resource for me.

The alignment of these supportive words and actions had a meaningful impact on this individual and their career.

Organizations that approach DEI as strategy can be successful—wildly successful. As the IBM case described at the beginning of this chapter suggests, carefully constructed, communicated, and integrated strategic efforts that begin with reflection on organizational purpose, goals, and SWOT have great potential for positive change.

Always, Always Target the Dismantling of Discrimination

We want the goals that you set for your organization to be lofty (and SMART). We want your organizations to thrive as workforces become more diverse. In Section 4, we present a more detailed examination of employment cycle and consider various ways that organizations can improve the way in which their diverse workforces work together. But before we end this section, we articulate that inherent in any organizational needs analysis and in considering the improvement of any workforce is an identification and dismantling of discriminatory policies that exist. If your organization has discriminatory policies, they simply must be acknowledged and removed. This is always an organizational need.

Jennifer Eberhardt's book, *Biased*, really hit home in reminding us how painstakingly obvious (but seemingly difficult) it can be to take actions to eliminate (or at least become aware of and reduce) bias.[13] In the book, she discusses Nextdoor, a company that operates a social network application of the same name that connects people in local neighborhoods throughout the United States. Nextdoor approached her because it had a racial profiling problem: Users who were looking for and sharing recommendations about people who render services occasionally posted comments such as a "suspicious Black man." Given that Jennifer realized this was part of implicit biases, she recommended that Nextdoor institute a delayed reporting that made people really think more deeply about their suspicions. Before reporting about suspicious people on Nextdoor's crime and safety tab, respondents now (before they report the ostensible activity) must go through a checklist of reminders that focus on the exact behavior the individual was doing rather than assuming criminality based on race. In addition, reports now must include a full description of clothing, build, and location (rather than just race and gender). The institution of this organizational policy curbed racial profiling by 75%.

As you think about leading your diverse workforce, recall that your actions can (and, it is hoped, will) have very large consequences in making organizational members reduce their discriminatory behaviors and work to create more equitable workplaces. It is critically important for ensuring that future organizations thrive as diversity increases by remembering that the dismantling of current discriminatory practices should always be at least one organizational goal.

---

[13] Eberhardt, J. (2019). *Biased: Uncovering the hidden prejudice that shapes what we see, think, and do.* Viking.

Tools for Working Together

Begin a SWOT analysis for your unit or organization. If we put a SWOT together with other tools we have, it might look like Figure 11.1.

Start with the following questions: What is the purpose of our unit? What is the function? Who is served? What are the core activities? Then ask, What is the desired outcome? What should people do and know? How should they behave? What are the deliverables? What percentage is desired? What is this end point? Next, ask, If we want to meet that end point, what are the specific goals? How do we set goals to get to that end point?

And then before you move ahead, consider whether the SWOT analysis informs your goals. Does it change any goals? Revise the achievable goals, and then set about achieving them.

Unit Name:

1) Purpose(s) of Unit:

2) Desired Focus/Outcome(s) (**NEEDS ANALYSIS**):

3) Specific Goals/Coordinated Actions to Achieve Desired Outcomes (**GOAL SETTING**):

4) SWOT Consideration(s) (**SWOT**) with particular attention to buy-in and costs

Strengths:	Weaknesses:
Opportunities:	Threats:

5) Revised but Still Specific Goals/Coordinated Actions to Achieve Desired Outcomes (**GOAL SETTING**):

Figure 11.1 Example of SWOT analysis worksheet.

SECTION 4

MUST DO'S FOR LEADING A DIVERSE WORKFORCE TOGETHER

Shortly after allegations of harassment emerged against Harvey Weinstein and other prominent men in the midst of the #MeToo movement, startup founder and chief executive officer Andrea Barrica wrote, "What's often ignored is that diversity is not only a pipeline or recruiting issue. It's an issue of making the people who do make it through the pipeline want to stay at your company." She went on to describe helpful tips to establishing and maintaining a code of conduct that could improve people's experiences in the pipeline, in recruitment, and ultimately as employees. Barrica called out what many leaders fail to fully recognize: Diversity, equity, and inclusion (DEI) matters at every stage of the talent management cycle, from recruitment to selection, from retention to promotion. Because these phases are inherently interconnected, effective DEI policies and practices must also be aligned.

We asked our class of diverse MBA students to reflect on the DEI initiatives that they have seen work well in organizations. They generated the following list of policies and practices that can help translate organizational strategy into change, including mentorship programs, accountability structures, training activities, support groups, and clear human resources processes:

- Mentorship support program and resources groups
- Policies, stipends, and performance indicators that can support these DEI initiatives
- Initiatives that make DEI conversations front and center seem to work.
- Initiatives that tie real dollar amounts to DEI efforts
- People pay attention to initiatives that lose them actual money.
- Hiring initiatives
- Implicit bias training
- Sponsorship
- Mentorship
- Exposure to senior leadership
- Efforts that seek to develop diverse employees into future leaders
- Diverse management teams and DEI committees
- Ally programs to support minorities inside the organization
- Clear rules for promotions
- Initiatives that celebrate our differences and allow for learning in an organic way
- Workshops specific to how it applies to our particular (not just generalized) workplace
- Implicit Association Test trainings specific to our workplace
- Having senior leaders be vocal about supporting DEI and actively making it known they are willing to sponsor underrepresented or minority groups in the workplace
- Educating people about the experiences and feelings of people in out-groups
- Teaching about actionable behaviors with the objectives in mind
- Proactive, not reactive, work
- Initiatives that make DEI a part of every action the company takes
- Start with a diverse team at the beginning

- More general bias training
- Wider recruiting school and/or organization targets
- Use of minority-focused networks
- Mentorship programs
- Education
- Employee resource groups
- Company-wide events that highlight underrepresented group members
- Acknowledgment of some group's struggles
- Maternity leave and accommodations for new mothers
- Work activities with random assignment to teams for an activity so we can experience having more (versus less) in common
- Affinity groups
- When there is a diverse HR team who believes in diversifying the company
- "Lunch and Learn" topics for everyone centered around awareness and current issues
- Woman and Minority-owned business certification entities
- I think cultural events at offices to celebrate major world festivals is really nice.
- I think mentorship is important and really helps.
- Diversity dialogues
- Required diversity training
- Clear and healthy organizational norms around DEI
- Mandatory trainings about DEI that are structured around workplace situations
- Employee safe spaces
- Initiatives that are woven into a company's overall strategic initiatives, rather than separately labeled as "DEI initiatives"
- Metrics-based approaches that include both top-down and bottom-up strategies
- Support groups
- Social events across different groups of peoples

- Sponsored collaboration boards
- Having leaders who reflect the workforce composition
- Solid, standardized hiring practices
- More diversity in our talent pipeline
- Events that are open to people in and outside of the diverse group
- Development initiatives within affinity groups (e.g., financial literacy, public speaking, etc.)

Which of these ideas represents best practice or best evidence? And how can they be integrated successfully in a talent management system? The chapters in this section address these questions and provide specific guidance for translating DEI strategy into practice.

12
The Attraction–Selection–Attrition Model Applied to Working Together

In July 2015, a Black woman in Texas was moments away from beginning a new job at her alma mater when she was pulled over by a police officer for failing to signal a lane change. She was found dead in a prison cell 3 days later. Had she lived, Sandra Bland would have likely taken the financial and emotional stress of the traffic stop with her to her new job; this single experience may have created hurdles in the way of her onboarding, socialization, and potentially her success in the new job. The circumstances of her death, and the public outcry that followed, impacted the psychological experience of many Black Americans.

The toll of this event and the deaths of Black people such as George Floyd and Breonna Taylor—intertwined with the racist history of policing in the United States—created circumstances in which many Black Americans wanted or needed to "call in Black" at work. One man blogged, "I am calling in Black because death is always a possible outcome when you are Black and come in contact with law enforcement. And if I have to live with that for the rest of my life, I am sure work can live without me for a day." Another woman explained that

> the other day when I was driving to work and I noticed water randomly pouring from my eyes, I realized something: I was grieving . . . watching the same narrative play out over and over again takes a toll. Sometimes, I need a minute.

And, acknowledging the critical role that workplaces play, another writer urged Black people to "take the personal day, sick day or whatever other day you can to unplug from forcing yourself to be part of spaces that don't affirm you." Of course, many people do not have the luxury of taking time off and instead had to go to work even while they were experiencing the pain and exhaustion exemplified by these quotes.

The ways that a single traffic stop might have affected Sandra Bland's individual work experience at her new job, and the events that instead unfolded and impacted millions of workers throughout the country, emphasize the permeability of the boundaries between life, work, and identities. Whether people are starting a new job or trying to move up the ladder, they are deeply affected by their identities. People can't take any identity "off at the door" when they get to work, and so, many are anxious for action. Many are tired of waiting for their organizations to look and feel different.

Yet, a *Harvard Business Review* article provocatively titled "Why Diversity Programs Fail"[1] is emblematic of a broader sense that traditional diversity, equity, and inclusion (DEI) efforts are not successfully transforming organizations. People want to "call in Black" partly because they do not feel seen, heard, or understood at work. There are many reasons why existing programs are not yielding the desired outcomes—beliefs are difficult to change, systemic structures perpetuate the status quo, and other crises can usurp resources. We focus on two barriers to change that organizational psychologists have identified as being particularly crucial.

First, as we've mentioned previously, a huge barrier to organizational change is a lack of support from top-level leaders. DEI efforts are less likely to be implemented, fully engaged, or sustained when leaders are not fully on board. Beliefs about diversity can sometimes be polarizing and can lead to debates and conflict. They can make people feel unwelcome, threatened, and pressured, and people sometimes react negatively to even the idea of such initiatives.

---

[1] Dobbin, F., & Kalev, A. (2016, July–August). Why diversity programs fail: And what works better. *Harvard Business Review.*

Top-level leaders have the opportunity to lead by example—not just talking the talk, but walking the walk. It is the leaders who set the norms of what is expected and what is unacceptable in an organization. It is the leaders who can leverage social, political, and financial capital to DEI efforts. It's one thing for a chief executive officer (CEO) to say "at our company, we treat everyone fairly." It's a whole different thing for a CEO to say "at our company, we value, celebrate, and respect all of the ways that we are different from each other. We strive to proactively counter prejudice in our teams, products, and communities" and then be an active participant in company-wide diversity programs.

Much more common than this transformational kind of leadership is a laissez-faire approach. DEI programs are sometimes relegated to the responsibility of human resource professionals. Leaders can and do point to initiatives that are happening, but they fail to directly engage in them. By abdicating responsibility to a unit (human resources) that is not often well-respected in organizations, leaders may be implicitly conveying a lack of genuine commitment to change. Or, leaders may emphasize inclusion but fail to devote meaningful resources to relevant initiatives.

Instead of standing in the way of change, leaders have the opportunity to model, normalize, and institutionalize inclusion. Sandra Bland was not at work when she was pulled over for failing to signal a lane change, but she could have been starting a new job 3 days later. The police officer who stopped her was at work. The officials in the prison where she died were at work. Millions of people who have read or seen accounts of the events of that July day work. Leaders will confront these realities at work. Leaders can create psychologically safe environments in which the blows of these realities might be softened.

A second major barrier to the effectiveness of DEI programs is inherent in their positioning. If DEI strategy focuses only on diversity training, or only on expanded recruitment, or only on performance management to create DEI, it is destined for disappointing returns. To consider DEI "programs" minimizes their critical strategic position. No single initiative can create the kind of change that people are seeking—no single program can create equity. Considerations for DEI have to filter through every aspect of an organization, through every personnel decision, and through every company message and event. To translate DEI strategy into action, policies and practices must be aligned across all aspects of talent and people management systems.

In his discussion of organizational culture, Dr. Ben Schneider summed it up succinctly: "The people make the place."[2] Organizations are indeed a reflection of the people who comprise them. The composition of organizations, Schneider further suggested, is a direct function of the systems of attraction, selection, and attrition (ASA). This ASA model emphasizes that an organization will be attractive to a particular kind of job-seeker, that the same kind of job-seeker is more likely to get selected for a particular organization, and that the same kinds of people will tend to stay in that organization.

Consider an organization that is known for a hostile, sexist, or harassing culture for women. Few women will consider applying for jobs at that organization, female job applicants will be seen as a "poor fit" for the organization and not hired, and even women who are hired may be likely to leave the organization. Over time, the ASA process would likely increase the homogeneity and decrease the diversity of such an organization; men would be attracted, selected, and retained, whereas women would be less attracted, less selected, and would leave. Thus, it is critical for DEI strategic goals to be reflected in thoughtful approaches for enhancing DEI in terms of increasing employee attraction, enhancing employee selection, and reducing employee attrition.

Tools for Working Together

Reflect on your current (or most recent) workplace and consider the following questions:

---

[2] Schneider, B. (1987). The people make the place. *Personnel Psychology, 40*(3), 437–453.

1. If the "people make the place," what kind of place is your organization?
2. To what extent are DEI efforts made across the talent management cycle, from recruitment to selection to retention?
3. To what extent are these efforts integrated versus separated?
4. Is there a clear and comprehensive DEI strategy driving these efforts? How might that strategy be improved?

13
Increasing Diversity, Equity, and Inclusion in Employee Attraction

Mikki and Eden work at an amazing university with incredible students, faculty, and staff. This university is located in the heart of Texas, a state which codified laws that substantially impact reproductive health care. This has a variety of implications not only for those of us who live and work in Texas but also for our institution and its future. How will organizations in Texas attract and recruit talent when people who are concerned about having access to lifesaving procedures for themselves and their family members may not be willing to work anywhere in the state?

Recruitment of women is now especially challenging for organizations in states such as ours, but organizations can and have responded to this challenge.

One visible response was that of Dick's Sporting Goods chief executive officer (CEO) Lauren Hobart, who used LinkedIn to declare that

> at DICK'S, our teammates are the heart of our business, and we are committed to protecting their health and well-being. Today, the Supreme Court announced a decision to overturn *Roe v. Wade*, removing the federal right to an abortion and leaving the decision up to each state. While we do not know what decision each state will make in response to this ruling, we at DICK'S Sporting Goods are prepared to ensure that all of our teammates have consistent and safe access to the benefits we provide, regardless of the state in which they live. In response to today's

ruling, we are announcing that if a state one of our teammates lives in restricts access to abortion, DICK'S Sporting Goods will provide up to $4,000 in travel expense reimbursement to travel to the nearest location where that care is legally available. This benefit will be provided to any teammate, spouse or dependent enrolled in our medical plan, along with one support person.

Such efforts may be essential for recruiting women in states such as Texas and for supporting diversity, equity, and inclusion (DEI) more generally.

An organization can only be as diverse and inclusive as the people who are willing to apply for jobs at the organization. If any group of people (e.g., women, Latinx people, and people with disabilities) don't apply, then they can't even *see* the table, much less take a seat at it. A more significant focus on recruitment efforts may be particularly necessary in light of research on the importance of a diverse pool of applicants.[1] In a convincing set of studies, researchers considered the likelihood that a woman would get chosen for a particular job depending on whether she was (a) the only woman in the pool with several other men or (b) one of several women in a pool with several other men. The article's title conveys its conclusion: "If There's Only One Woman in Your Candidate Pool, There's Statistically No Chance She'll Be Hired."[2]

The reason for this is that when there's just one woman in the candidate pool, it looks like that woman is a social token. It's inferred that she is just there because she is a woman. In contrast, having multiple women conveys a social norm. The norm that is learned from having multiple women in the candidate pool is that the company already employs many highly qualified women. This finding about women is likely to extend to people from a variety of marginalized backgrounds; increasing the diversity of the candidate pool is hugely important for ensuring DEI. This means that careful attention to the

---

[1] Johnson, S. K., Hekman, D. R., & Chan, E. T. (2016, April 26). If there's only one woman in your candidate pool, there's statistically no chance she'll be hired. *Harvard Business Review*.
[2] Johnson, S. K., Hekman, D. R., & Chan, E. T. (2016, April 26). If there's only one woman in your candidate pool, there's statistically no chance she'll be hired. *Harvard Business Review*.

ways that DEI intersects with the recruitment process in its broadest sense—the process of increasing the attractiveness of the organization to potential employees—is critical for organizations.

Review Recruitment Tools and Strategies

A good starting point is to review existing recruitment tools and strategies. Make a list: What is your organization already doing to increase its attractiveness to employees? What kinds of images are on the website? How are job ads written? Where are they placed? Who talks to potential applicants (and who doesn't)? Where do recruiters go (and where don't they go)?

Once the list is written, look at it again with two questions in mind: To what extent will these strategies be attractive to job candidates from a variety of backgrounds? and To what extent will these strategies be attractive to job candidates who will contribute to inclusion? You can evaluate these questions through small group discussion and reflection, but it may also be helpful to bring in data for guidance. Particularly relevant data might include the proportion of applicants for different jobs who are from marginalized backgrounds; if you see that women, for example, make up a small percentage of applicants for a given job, it might help you focus discussion on strategies to improve the recruitment of women. The goal of this analysis should be to identify opportunities for positive change. Next, we describe specific approaches that will help achieve this.

Strategically Located Recruitment

One way to ensure or increase diversity in the recruitment process is to engage in enhanced or targeted recruitment. Diverse applicant pools aren't magically going to emerge just by listing a job on LinkedIn. Proactive strategies that place carefully constructed job advertisements in outlets, locations, and social networks where they

Increasing DEI in Employee Attraction

Figure 13.1 Websites depicting Black versus White employees.

will be seen by people from a variety of backgrounds will be more effective. It can help to broaden the educational institutions, organizations, and professional organizations at which jobs are advertised to include historically Black colleges and universities, minority-owned organizations, and professional organizations that are geared toward marginalized people.

Project Authentic DEI Optics

One process that organizations should enact when they're trying to attract people from different backgrounds in their applicant pool is to thoughtfully construct how their organizations look to the outside world and, especially, to the people from marginalized backgrounds that they're trying to attract. These optics matter, and they can be found on a variety of materials, brochures, and/or web pages. In a study conducted in our lab,[3] we examined potential applicants' interest in companies based on the manipulation of a website. The only thing that differed between the websites they viewed was whether it included a picture of a White employee or an employee from an ethnic minority background (Figure 13.1). Black and Latinx participants indicated that they were more attracted to organizations with ethnically diverse versus White employees depicted.

---

[3] Avery, D., Hernandez, M., & Hebl, M. (2004). Who's watching the race? Racial salience in recruitment advertising. *Journal of Applied Social Psychology, 34,* 146–161.

Our research also found that White participants were equally attracted to both types of organizations. These kinds of optics also exist in the breakdown of who serves as leaders on panels, as visitors and guest speakers, and as experts. Consistent, visible markers of diversity signal that an organization notices, values, and affirms diversity. Optics matter.

But there is a critical caveat: When organizations try to improve their optics, it's not going to be effective if the way that they present themselves to applicants is just "window dressing" or if images are inaccurate reflections of what really exists within the organizations. Instead, organizational materials should truly reflect the company's objectives and reality. If DEI is a goal but not yet a reality, it may be important to reflect that carefully. In our own department, we worked with a committee to compose a description that reflects both the goal and the reality:

> It is [our] expressed mission . . . to actively counter prejudice and discrimination. . . . We understand that this missacknowledgeion must go beyond a statement alone; thus, we emphasize this statement as a first step to guide our subsequent words, actions, decision-making, and corrective measures. We aim to become a department that consistently engages in learning about the experiences of marginalized groups, actively supports the inclusion and development of all, and remains ready and willing to acknowledge mistakes or missteps we have made and will make along this path of improvement.

We specifically constructed this language in acknowledgment of the fact that our department does not yet reflect our ideals of diversity or inclusion—we understand that we still have a ways to go, and we are committed to continuing to prioritize positive change.

Explicit Communication About Diversity Recruitment

Words matter. Communicating support for some features of diversity—such as sexual orientation diversity, neurodiversity, and ability diversity—is more difficult to illustrate visually than other features of diversity. The words that organizations use in describing their employees, their DEI strategy, and jobs themselves can be important in the attraction phase of talent management.

From a strategic standpoint, companies tend to take one of two general approaches that are communicated in their formal values, mission, or objectives statements. The first is an identity-conscious strategy, which emphasizes that differences between employees are acknowledged, embraced, and celebrated. The second is an identity-blind strategy, which instead emphasizes that all employees are treated the same regardless of their identity. There are advantages and disadvantages to both approaches, but overall, research suggests that identity-conscious statements are more appealing to people from diverse backgrounds. People from historically marginalized groups are more attracted to organizations that recognize and meaningfully include their different perspectives.

Consider the following statement from Walmart:

> At Walmart, we believe we're best equipped to help our associates, customers, and the communities we serve live better when we really know them. That means understanding, respecting, and valuing diversity, unique styles, experiences, identities, ideas and opinions, while being inclusive of all people.

This identity-conscious perspective signals to prospective employees something meaningfully different than a standard, identity-blind statement:

> We are an Equal Opportunity/Affirmative Action Employer with commitment to diversity at all levels, and considers for employment qualified applicants without regard to race, color, religion, age, sex, sexual orientation, gender identity, national or ethnic origin, genetic information, disability or protected veteran status.

The former sounds more like it's from an organization that's working toward inclusion; the latter sounds like it's from an organization worried about fulfilling a legal requirement.

Implicit Communication About Diversity Recruitment

Sometimes the words that are used to describe not only the company as a whole but also a particular job can influence the diversity of the applicant pool. Research has shown that some organizations commit very flagrant biases in the gender pronouns that they use in their job descriptions. For instance, they might advertise that "*he* will know how to operate the equipment" or "*she* will provide assistance to the CEO."

In addition to using overtly gendered pronouns, some organizations advertise their jobs with descriptions including gendered titles. Examples include positional names such as foreman, fireman, craftsman, chairman, salesman, waitress, weatherman, and handyman. One visible example of this was the U.S. Marine Corps, which listed in job descriptions the titled positions of "basic infantryman," "manpower officer," "first support man," "wireman," and "reconnaissance man." Although it removed 16 of such gendered job titles in 2016, it did leave in place "rifleman" and "mortarman."

Biases in job descriptions also include the use of strong gender stereotypes. Masculine stereotypes are evident in job descriptions that describe the ideal candidate as "a strong employee" or as someone who "thrives in a competitive atmosphere" and is "assertive." Feminine stereotypes are evident in job descriptions recruiting employees who "are community concerned," have a "polite and pleasant style," and can "nurture and connect with customers."

Such a microscopic look at word choices may seem far too nuanced, and yet there are a growing number of studies showing the impact that subtle word choices can have on the application pool.[4,5] Language in your job posting can predict the gender

---

[4] Gaucher, D., Friesen, J., & Kay, A. C. (2011). Evidence that gendered wording in job advertisements exists and sustains gender inequality. *Journal of Personality and Social Psychology, 101*(1), 109–128. https://doi.org/10.1037/a0022530.

[5] Oldford, E., & Fiset, J. (2021). Decoding bias: Gendered language in finance internship job postings. *Journal of Behavioral and Experimental Finance, 31*, 100544.

diversity of the applicant pool and ultimately the gender diversity of those selected. Job descriptions for male-dominated occupations use many more masculine words than those for gender-neutral or female-dominated occupations. Fortunately, there are tools (e.g., software programs) that can be used to detect such patterns of gendered language. If analyses suggest potential differences, then organizations can either remove the words and replace them with more neutral words or try to use the same number of masculine, feminine, and gender-neutral descriptors and verbs. Overall, it may be helpful to reconsider and rework job descriptions to (a) be fully aligned with the requirements of the job and (b) remove or replace any potentially biasing language.

Using Supportive Policies to Attract Workers

One way to attract diverse employees to an organization is to institute and advertise policies that appeal to a variety of people. These can be policies that are primarily helpful to a particular group of people (e.g., child care subsidies, which would be most appealing to parents of young children) or to a broader population(e.g., stipends for care needs in general or compressed work weeks). As examples, we briefly describe policies that might appeal to people with care responsibilities, people with disabilities, and people from a variety of religious backgrounds.

With regard to family-friendly policies, the possibilities are enormous. Companies could offer flextime, flexplace, job sharing, part-time work, parental leave, lactation support programs, elder care or child care subsidies or on-site options, flexible emergency leave, tuition subsidy programs for educational endeavors, and/or employee assistance programs. These are precisely the kinds of programs that are beginning to take hold with top *Fortune* 500 companies in an effort to support and retain diverse workers. For instance, Hewlett Packard, is a leader not only in the computer industry but also in supporting working parents. The company has created a set of benefits that it refers to as "HPE Work That Fits Your

Life,"[6] which includes (a) a minimum of 6 months fully paid leave for parents after the birth or adoption of a child, (b) transition support for parents who want to return to work part-time up to 3 years post birth or adoption of a child, (c) the opportunity for employees to leave early once a month on Fridays to take time for themselves, (d) transition support for those retiring by offering part-time work, and (e) training for people who left the workforce (e.g., mothers who took time off to care for their children) but are returning to the workforce. Netflix offers the highest amount of paid leave (52 weeks), but Lululemon (26 weeks), Hewlett Packard (26 weeks), Etsy (26 weeks), and Dropbox (24 weeks) all offer considerable amounts of paid leave for mothers and fathers.

These policies are particularly important in the context of the United States, which is the only industrialized nation that does not offer federally mandated paid parental leave or provide substantial support for early child care needs. But study after study shows the importance of these kinds of policies, not only for the well-being of families but also in the interest of organizational outcomes. In fact, a whopping 69% of fathers and 66% of mothers would change jobs if they could get additional weeks or months of time to care for their children.[7] The COVID-19 pandemic particularly highlighted the problem of missing child care infrastructure: Many women who worked in child care centers and elementary education did not return to work because they did not have the help that they needed with their own children.[8]

Providing support for people with disabilities might also help enhance DEI in the recruitment process. People with disabilities are a very underutilized, underemployed segment of the population; many who

---

[6] May, A. (2019, April 30). *Leading the way in workplace flexibility*. Hewlett Packard Enterprise. https://www.hpe.com/us/en/newsroom/blog-post/2019/04/leading-the-way-in-workplace-flexibility.html.

[7] Promundo. (2018). *Helping dads care*. https://promundoglobal.org/wp-content/uploads/2018/06/Promundo-DMC-Helping-Men-Care-Report_FINAL.pdf.

[8] Collins, C., Ruppanner, L., & Scarborough, W. J. (2021, November 8). Why haven't U.S. mothers returned to work. The child-care infrastructure they need is still missing. *The Washington Post*. https://www.washingtonpost.com/politics/2021/11/08/why-havent-us-mothers-returned-work-child-care-infrastructure-they-need-is-still-missing.

are not working would like to work. Policies such as the option to work from home or providing specialized equipment, in addition to greater emphasis on accessibility in all communication, might improve the attractiveness of an organization. How many job advertisements specify that American Sign Language interpreters are available for interviews? How many organizational websites are carefully constructed to be easily interpreted by people with visual disabilities? And, importantly, what could it change if your company considered such actions?

Similarly, employers will also attract more diverse applicants by considering the needs of people from a variety of religious backgrounds. Recognizing and valuing the beliefs, holidays, and traditions of people from diverse religions can in fact begin in the recruitment process. It would help to indicate that no interviews would be expected during religious activities (e.g., holidays and sacred times such as worship services or Sabbath). It would also be helpful to be sensitive to dietary restrictions and to limit alcohol-related activities that may be prohibited in some religious faiths. Providing and communicating about quiet spaces for prayer and/or meditation may also help signal the organization's commitment to DEI.

Many of these policies would be attractive to the overwhelming majority of potential job applicants. Indeed, research suggests that these policies are particularly attractive to people who might use them, but they are also viewed favorably by people who do not expect to need them. Organizations that are creative, flexible, and generous in their supportive policies will find that they are rewarded with a stronger talent pool.

Tools for Working Together

Reflect on your current (or most recent) workplace and consider the following questions:

1. Where are the typical places that your organization recruits new applicants? How might you alter or enhance recruiting efforts to get a more diverse set of applicants?

2. What policies does your organization currently have that are appealing to applicants? Are there ones that are missing and badly needed? How might you advocate for these?
3. Which employee attraction strategies do you think could be implemented that are realistic in the context of this organization?

14
Enhancing Diversity, Equity, and Inclusion in Employee Selection

Recently, we had a conversation with a prominent professor from a business school well outside the top 10. We remarked that the business school might do well by their diverse student body to hire more professors who were women and/or came from underrepresented groups. We pointed out a couple of influential scholars who were from marginalized backgrounds, who had dozens of top-tier publications, and who would certainly entertain an offer from the said business school. Several of our suggestions were known as superstars in the field. They even applied for the open position at this business school but were routinely rejected without even getting an interview. (Fortunately, the scholars from marginalized backgrounds were offered several excellent jobs *elsewhere* throughout the country.)

Our colleague retorted that they were looking for professors from the top schools such as Harvard and Wharton, and he further rationalized that the particular areas of expertise of the scholars who were from underrepresented groups were not of interest to the school. In the end, the business school hired a new professor who, instead of having dozens of outstanding publications, had a degree from an elite institution. We learned later from another business school colleague that the practice of having professors with degrees from such elite places gives the school bragging rights that it can then use in recruiting students.

This conversation was frustrating for two reasons. First, the selection criteria appear to be very unfair. Who applies to and attends premiere business schools? Many people who go to business school must attend local institutions because of finances, family, and other restrictive decisions. If second-tier business schools are making such restrictions, are individuals who don't go to top schools only eligible for jobs at the lowest rungs of business schools throughout the country? The profound loss of talent is immeasurable. Second, my colleague spoke matter-of-factly, without compunction. In 2022, his elitism along with assuredly sexist and racist connotations were acceptable cornerstones of his selection strategy. This is how organizations and institutions fail to embody diversity, equity, and inclusion (DEI). They isolate themselves and hold on to norms that stifle progress.

How can inclusive leaders counteract these kinds of belief systems and biases that are embedded in job decision-making? How do we ensure that our employee selection is free of bias? Or, more generally, how do we enhance the quality of our employee selection? We next describe best practice and evidence for reducing bias in employee selection. These are policies and practices that can be enacted in support of an integrated DEI strategy in the selection phase of the talent management process.

Defining Job Criteria a Priori

One of the most important ways to maximize the selection of a diverse workforce is to define job criteria a priori. This means to articulate up front, or in advance of choosing any candidate, what is necessary for someone to do a job well. So what knowledge and specific sets of skills and abilities does a person need to do the job? If these competencies can be carefully specified up front, this can guide the attention and evaluation of decision-makers in a manner that is fairer (and accurate).

Freelance journalist Rebecca Knight summarizes practical considerations for reducing bias in the hiring process.[1] These

---

[1] Knight, R. (2017, June 12). Seven practical ways to reduce bias in your hiring process. *Harvard Business Review*.

suggestions speak directly to the issue of specifying job criteria up front and before choosing applicants:

1. More of something is not always better. If a job requirement is 5 years of experience, an individual with 15 years of experience should not be viewed as being necessarily better than someone with 5 years. If they are, write that into the criteria. If they are not, judge them both as exceeding threshold. Sometimes getting "more" reflects privilege and access; more does not necessarily yield the best talent.
2. "Fit" is not a qualification for hiring. Fit is often a very vague, ambiguous term that people justify by saying that "they know it when they see it." If people are hired for "fit," this almost always involves embracing the status quo and reducing, rather than increasing, diversity. Instead, follow management scholar and influential thinker Adam Grant's advice to think about culture *add* (what a person will add to the organization) rather than culture *fit*.[2]
3. Think carefully about whether likability is critical for the job. Just because we like a candidate does not mean that they are actually qualified. This is particularly important given the "similar-to-me" bias[3] that leads us to like people who are similar to us and thus reduces diversity.

These cognitive traps reinforce the notion that we can and must reduce bias by first deciding what specific competencies are needed for a job and then assessing those (and only those) competencies.

---

[2] Schawbel, D. (2016, February 2). Adam Grant: Why you shouldn't hire for cultural fit. *Fortune.* https://www.forbes.com/sites/danschawbel/2016/02/02/adam-grant-why-you-shouldnt-hire-for-cultural-fit/?sh=3393bee97eba.
[3] Lin, T.-r., Dobbins, G. H., & Farh, J.-L. (1992). A field study of race and age similarity effects on interview ratings in conventional and situational interviews. *Journal of Applied Psychology, 77*(3), 363–371. https://doi.org/10.1037/0021-9010.77.3.363.

Conduct Identity-Hidden Reviews When Possible

Recall the well-known labor market study examining discrimination we described in Chapter 6:[4] Job applicants with the names Lakisha and Jamal do not get the same number of callbacks as otherwise identical applicants Emily and Greg. When possible, organizations can reduce such biases in selection systems by conducting identity-hidden reviews. What are identity-hidden applications? They are situations in which the demographic information about candidates remains hidden, so people who are selecting candidates do not see the names Emily, Greg, Lakisha, or Jamal. Those doing the selecting don't know the applicants' race, age, or other demographic characteristics.

Identity-hidden reviews and interviews attempt to level the playing field by focusing attention on candidates' specific qualifications and talents, rather than on surface demographic characteristics. The power of identity-hidden reviews was demonstrated in a study on improving the representation of female musicians in symphony orchestras. This work was done in response to the persistent underrepresentation of women in these positions to explore the potential role of biases in the review process. With the goal of removing gender as a factor in the audition process, the experimenters allowed reviewers to hear—but not see—the musical performances of applicants. The musicians were placed behind a screen for their audition. When gender was not observable—when gender was hidden behind the screen—women were more likely to be hired. The widespread implementation of this process ultimately resulted in much greater representation of female musicians.

Removing the names and other demographic cues that allow employers to focus more fairly on what each person brings to the table seems like it might be time-intensive. However, software

---

[4] Bertrand, M., & Mullainathan, S. (2004). Are Emily and Greg more employable than Lakisha and Jamal? A field experiment on labor market discrimination. *American Economic Review, 94*(4), 991–1013. doi:10.1257/0002828042002561.

programs are available that can systematically remove identifying information from applications.[5] Such processes for reviewing applications and resumes could help organizations improve the chances of hiring the very most qualified.

Yet, an important caveat should also be considered in the context of identity-hidden reviews. Music critic Anthony Tommasini[6] opined that "To Make Orchestras More Diverse, End Blind Auditions." In the context of the persistent underrepresentation of Black musicians and the racial reckoning of 2019, he wrote, "If the musicians onstage are going to better reflect the diversity of the communities they serve, the audition process has to be altered to take into fuller account artists' backgrounds and experiences. Removing the screen is a crucial step." He further reminded readers that

> blind auditions are based on an appealing premise of pure meritocracy: An orchestra should be built from the very best players, period. But ask anyone in the field, and you'll learn that over the past century of increasingly professionalized training, there has come to be remarkably little difference between players at the top tier.

Comparing orchestra auditions to college admissions for Ivy League schools, he suggested that schools and orchestras should "move past those marks, embrace diversity as a social virtue and assemble a freshman class that advances other values along with academic achievement," which might include

> talent as an educator, interest in unusual repertoire or willingness to program innovative chamber events as well as pure musicianship. American orchestras should be able to foster these values, and a diverse complement of musicians, rather than passively waiting for representation to emerge from behind the audition screen.

---

[5] Heaslip, E. (2022, August 26). *The complete guide to blind hiring in 2021*. Vervoe. https://vervoe.com/blind-hiring.

[6] Tommasini, A. (2021). To make orchestras more diverse, end blind auditions. *The New York Times*. https://www.nytimes.com/2020/07/16/arts/music/blind-auditions-orchestras-race.html.

It may be worthwhile to integrate identity-hidden elements in a selection process that also includes an identity-conscious process through which other values are considered.

Consider Unorthodox Applicants

How does an assistant professor of architecture (2009) get hired as a dean of architecture (2010) in just one year? Someone was thinking outside the box. That's exactly what happened when it came to Dr. Sarah Whiting, a beloved dean who served at Rice University for 9 years. It's fairly unheard of to promote someone so junior to a dean position, but soon after she arrived at Rice, it became clear that she was someone special. She made an impact by serving on many different committees and ventures across campus and the community, and she was recognized as educator of the year by four different architectural organizations across a 4-year period. No surprise, she has moved on and is serving as dean of a prominent university.[7]

Employers often rely on their stereotypes for what it means to be a good employer (e.g., "think manager—think male"[8]) and then hire accordingly. One of our MBA students noted the potential unfairness of such presumptions by questioning whether it is fair to make comparisons between applicants who could afford private schools, tutoring, and Ivy League degrees and those who went to public schools:

> On paper, one looks better than the other but the kid from the state school has had more challenges and is used to facing adversity. I do not think it is fair that he does not get a shot or that there are jobs he should never get access to because he did not go to a certain school.

---

[7] New dean for graduate school design. (2019, April 17). *The Harvard Gazette*.
[8] Schein, V. E., Mueller, R., Lituchy, T., & Liu, J. (1996). Think manager—think male: A global phenomenon? *Journal of Organizational Behavior, 17*(1), 33–41.

Employers may tend to select those who went through a very traditional type of training, who put time in rank, who had a particular major, who went to an elite school, and/or who had a particular kind of internship. But employers often err when they use these kinds of indicators as sole proxies for the competencies that are required for a particular job. Excellent talent doesn't just come from any one indicator, and many things we think are important actually are not.

Sometimes employers also prefer those who have uninterrupted tenure or no "holes" or "gaps" in their resumes. But there are many reasons a person might take time off, some of which could make them an even stronger employee and many of which have no bearing on their performance at all. Does taking a break in paid employment to earn a new degree, travel internationally, or have a baby really matter in terms of the competencies that are required for a particular job?

Women in particular are affected by this tenure heuristic for several reasons. First, women tend to take on-roads and off-roads in their careers, mostly because they are the caregiving parent and the caregiving spouse. An article by Kapadia[9] and Figure 14.1 depict how such differences create the stubborn wealth gap between men and women. An examination of one's cumulative life earnings reveals that after taking into account off-roads that many women take, there is ultimately a caregiver tax of more than $1 million. That is, women (but not men) tend to experience three flat epochs in their lifetimes. The first time is when they become parents, the second time is when their own parents need looking after (elder care), and the third time is when they are taking care of their aging spouse (as women live longer). But the sum of these three experiences results in a lifetime gap at retirement of more than $1 million. These differences may be exacerbated even more when considering that many women raise children on their own.

---

[9] Kapadia, R. (2018, April 18). The stubborn wealth gap between men and women. *Barron's*. https://www.barrons.com/articles/the-stubborn-wealth-gap-between-men-and-women-1524099601.

Over a lifetime of savings, a women who takes three breaks from her career to care for children, parents, and a spouse can end up with a total of $1 million less in financial resources than men who have continuously stayed in the workforce.

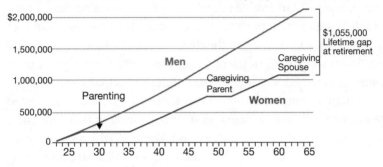

Figure 14.1 Cumulative lifetime earnings for men versus women.
Source: Bank of America Merrill Lynch/Age Wave.

Second, the experiences that women have are valued differently than the experiences that men have. Researchers found that women who travel internationally are perceived as doing so for pleasure and enjoyment, whereas men are perceived as learning new skills and expanding their networks.[10] Thus, a gap in time may be interpreted for men as adding to their career skills, whereas for women, it is perceived as simply vacationing. Uninterrupted tenure should not be a necessary heuristic for good hiring decisions.

Another problematic heuristic is that selection decisions may overvalue the name recognition of prior employers. When applicants have mid-level experiences at well-known *Fortune* 500 companies, they can be seen as more appealing to employers than applicants who hold higher level positions at companies with less name recognition. These latter positions may actually require more initiative, innovation, and flexibility, but they are not valued as much because the names of the organizations may be less salient.

Each of these biases gets in the way of hiring the best candidates; hence, organizations should consider unorthodox applicants. This means looking beyond traditional measures of success. Applicants

---

[10] Valian, V. (1997). *Why so slow? The advancement of women.* MIT Press.

who do not go to fancy schools, who have worked for small or family-owned businesses, who have not worked or followed the traditional path, or who have gathered valuable experience in a variety of contexts may be exactly the kinds of employees who will perform best in a given job. If you focus on an ideal candidate as someone who knows multiple languages, who has an adaptive mindset, or who has substantial leadership experience, this may point you in a direction away from Ivy Leaguers who interned at a *Fortune* 500 company. By looking beyond traditional notions of success at unorthodox candidates, you find new and exciting pools of high-potential talent.

Use Structured Interviews

Structured interviews comprise standardized sets of questions used to formally assess the fit of a job candidate to the criterion needed to perform a particular job. They provide each candidate with the same set of questions and similar set of experiences; the structure and questions asked are often empirically tied to the qualities that are shown to be effective in doing the job well. Furthermore, structured interviews demonstrate that an organization is committed to a fair process. Compare the structured interview to an unstructured interview in which questions are asked as they arise, the interviewer often talks more than the applicant, and personality and fit seem to weigh more than qualifications (Box 14.1). In short, structured interviews are a game-changer. Organizations that are trying to practice unbiased selection procedures should absolutely rely on the use of structured interviews. A very large body of research suggests that structured interviews are one of the known ways to increase the fairness and effectiveness of the selection process.[11]

Google's publicly available re:Work[12] resources synthesize some of the best practice and evidence regarding people management,

---

[11] Bohnet, I. (2016, April 18). How to take the bias out of interviews. *Harvard Business Review*.

[12] re:Work. (2021). *Guide: Use of structured interviews*. https://rework.withgoogle.com/guides/hiring-use-structured-interviewing/steps/introduction.

> **Box 14.1 Unstructured and Structured Interview Questions**
>
> Unstructured Interview Questions
>
> > What can you tell me about yourself?
> > What do you like to do in your spare time?
> > What is your single most proud accomplishment?
> > What is your ideal job?
> > Why do you want this job?
> > What are your greatest strengths and weaknesses?
>
> Structured Interview Questions
>
> > Tell me about a time in which you were very effective at [a critical job task they will be doing].
> > Suppose a stressful experience [describe one common with the job] happened. What precise steps would you take?
> > Suppose you had an interaction like this [describe in detail something they might encounter]. How would you approach it?
> > How do you run this [piece of equipment, machinery, test, something they will definitely need to know]? What is the exact experience you have had in doing this before?
> > Can you tell me about an ethical issue that you had to deal with at your last place of work and how you handled that?

including structured interviews. Structured interviews are interviews in which job applicants are asked the same set of questions as other applicants, and clear criteria are used to judge all applicants' responses. If the same questions and criteria are used for each applicant, there is then the belief that variations in the candidate assessment will reveal who is the best candidate. And this process is believed to be one of the fairest types of interview strategies. Structured interviews provide a systematic method through which to focus on the competencies that are needed for a job and to avoid bringing in extraneous information that could unfairly influence evaluations.

The approach that re:Work describes includes four components:

1. Using vetted, high-quality questions that are relevant to the role (no brainteasers!)
2. Recording comprehensive feedback of candidate answers so evaluators can easily review responses
3. Scoring with standardized rubrics so that all reviewers have a shared understanding of what a good, mediocre, and poor response looks like
4. Providing interviewer training and calibration so that interviewers are confident and consistent in their assessments

These features help ensure that each candidate gets the same opportunity to convey their competence for the job.

Get Behavioral Samples

Most people are surprised to find out that an *unstructured* interview is actually a pretty bad predictor of job performance. Some hiring managers (and many of us) just like to "go with their gut feeling" or "decide on the handshake" because they think that they can get an accurate impression of a person that tells them more than any interview answer could. But it turns out that if we want the best sense of an employee's behavior on the job, it helps to look at actual behavior.

One way to get behavioral samples that reflect how people will perform in a particular job and in a specific organization is through programs in which people are hired on a temporary basis (e.g., internships and temporary job rotation programs). From a selection standpoint, this can be an incredibly valuable source of information regarding potential talent. However, this may not be as appealing from a recruitment standpoint: People want and deserve more job security than a temporary position often allows.

Another strategy for observing behavior is to use a selection method called an assessment center. Assessment centers usually require candidates to engage in a variety of job-related tasks, such as being involved in a leaderless group activity, having to complete an in-basket or job sample task, or giving a presentation. These kinds of procedures can be time- and cost-intensive, so they are generally used for selection to high-level leadership positions.

This type of job sample task was (inadvertently) exactly what Mikki experienced when she went on the academic job market and met with Dean Bob Stein during an on-campus visit. The 45-minute meeting was supposed to be a fairly formal and traditional conversation about start-up needs and job details. Instead, the dean started a conversation about a data analysis he had run earlier in the day. When Mikki asked a question about it (mostly to show polite interest), he pulled out the data set and asked how she would interpret it. Thankfully, Mikki was able to interpret it accurately and give some feedback. She had delivered a sample of the type of behavior she would typically be engaging in as an assistant professor. On the one hand, this was a stressful, unexpected interview interaction. On the other hand, one might argue that it was a great way to get a sense of a candidate's job-relevant skills. He asked the candidate to perform a task relevant to her job, which is to look at a data set and try to interpret it.

A process that requires less time and cost, but is also a bit more removed from on-the-job behavior, is to integrate behavioral-based questions in the structured interview process. This involves asking questions that start with "Tell me about a time . . ." and end with a competency that is relevant to the job, such as ". . . you had to help your subordinates resolve a work-related conflict." Situational questions that start with prompts such as "What would you do if . . ." can also be useful in judging the extent to which candidates understand what they should do in a given situation that is relevant to the job. The extent to which the selection process can assess actual behaviors that are relevant to the job using any one of these methods will improve DEI and talent management more generally.

Focus on Metrics

Venture capitalist John Doerr titled his book, *Measure What Matters*.[13] His focus was on the ways that metrics can motivate goal-directed behavior, but this phrase has wide relevance to people and organizations. Organizations should maximize their focus on metrics whenever they can, and we particularly discuss this in the context of selection, evaluation, and potential promotion up the corporate ladder. Essentially, the more open-ended and subjective the criteria, the more likely they are to be biased. So instead, what organizations should do is create a rubric for evaluations across the talent management system.

In the context of employee selection specifically, this means that any knowledge, skill, or ability that is deemed to be important for performance in a job should be measured carefully. This begins with specifying the content of what will be measured, or which competencies should be assessed based on the a priori process described previously. It further requires that the evaluation of these competencies involves several best practices in assessment, such as (a) clear rating scales with behavioral anchors when possible (indicating what a rating of a "1" versus a "7" looks like in terms of behaviors), (b) required rater training (helping raters get understanding about which behaviors to assess and how they should be evaluated), (c) systems of accountability that motivate accuracy (requiring people to explain or justify their ratings helps avoid automatic biases), and (d) checks for consistency within and between raters (to ensure that people are making similar evaluations). Organizations that implement each of these strategies in the selection phase of the talent management process will have clear advantages in creating and sustaining DEI.

---

[13] Doerr, J. (2018). *Measure what matters: How Google, Bono, and the Gates Foundation rock the world with OKRs*. Penguin..

Tools for Working Together

Reflect on your current (or most recent) workplace.

1. Which of the selection strategies does your company already use?
2. Which does it not use?
3. What recommendations would you make to your company, given what you have just learned?

Watch the video titled "3 Things You Should Know About Workplace Gender Bias" by Iris Bohnet at https://www.youtube.com/watch?v=7bHoc1TW_Ps&ab_channel=HarvardKennedySchool. Consider some of the things that you can do to de-bias your own organization.

Visit the Google re:Work website at https://rework.withgoogle.com/guides/hiring-use-structured-interviewing/steps/introduction to learn about conducting structured interviews. Here, you will find information about the components involved in a structured interview, defining hiring attributes of appeal, drafting interview questions, understanding behavioral versus hypothetical questions, and using a grading rubric. You will also learn about Google's internal research.

15
Reducing Employee Attrition

At the beginning of the COVID-19 pandemic, Laura Danger[1] was a mother of both a 9-month-old and a 3-year-old in day care full-time. She was also an elementary schoolteacher in the Chicago Public School System working with third through sixth graders who had special needs. Because the United States has no mandatory paid leave for parents, she was forced to juggle. She taught classes online and shared child care with her dual-career husband. One solution, a stay-at-home nanny, proved to be too expensive. As their sick time got used up, her husband and Laura, particularly, became even more stressed out and had to go on short-term disability. Laura's case is not unique.

During the COVID-19 pandemic, people resigned from their current jobs in large numbers. Anthony Klotz, an associate professor at the University College of London, refers to this time period as "The Great Resignation."[2] Some estimates cite that more than half of people were searching for new jobs.[3] When asked, many of them stated that they are exhausted, they don't feel like they are valued, they don't feel like they belong, they want increased flexibility, they want better work–life balance, and they want more from their

---

[1] Kaplan, J. (2022, January 23). Meet a mom and teacher who hasn't been able to work because childcare is so unpredictable: "I was way behind on work and completely stressed, not sleeping." *Business Insider.* https://www.businessinsider.com/meet-mom-teacher-leaving-workforce-childcare-pandemic-paid-leave-2022-1.

[2] Klotz, A. (2022, June 3). *The great resignation is still here, but whether it stays is up to leaders.* The Forum Network. https://www.oecd-forum.org/posts/the-great-resignation-is-still-here-but-whether-it-stays-is-up-to-leaders.

[3] Foster, S. (2021, August 23). *Survey: 55% of Americans expect to search for a new job over the next 12 months.* Bankrate. https://www.bankrate.com/personal-finance/job-seekers-survey-august-2021.

employers. Another term that people are using to describe the way that they are coping with their job frustration, burnout, or feeling of inequity is to "quiet quit."[4] Quiet quitting refers to the idea that a worker do just the minimum amount of work that is required for a job and not go above that physically, psychologically, or emotionally in any way. A Gallup poll suggested that 50% of the workforce quietly quit on some level in 2022.[5] It is not clear how much overlap there is between those who took part in quiet quitting and those who took part in the Great Resignation, but one thing is clear: Issues of attrition have never been so important to our workforce. And these issues are even more complex when considering the potential exodus of a diverse workforce.

In Chapters 13 and 14, we discussed how to attract and select a more diverse group of employees to join an organization. But is it enough to just get people *into* an organization? How do we ensure that these employees from diverse backgrounds are going to stay and won't leave our organization? What strategies can we adopt to maximize the likelihood of employees not only staying but also moving up through the pipeline? It is critically important that we focus attention on how employees are treated once they are in organizations.

The necessity of this attention is clear from the comments of one of our Black MBA students who stated that he worked with a senior recruiter who was in charge of diversity recruiting. When he asked her why she did the work, she said it was because she enjoyed quantifying her wins in work ("If she increases female hiring by 10%, then her company wins awards for being women-friendly"). Although she hired diverse applicants, the recruiter was very difficult to work with and not very supportive of these same people she hired. Our student questioned, "What is the point of recruiting diverse talent if they come to an environment they do not want to stay in?"

---

[4] Kaplan, J. (2022, September 11). How to "act your wage," according to 2 millennials who did it: "If a company is paying you, let's say minimum wage, you're gonna put in minimum effort." *Business Insider*. https://www.businessinsider.com/how-act-your-wage-quiet-quit-work-less-get-paid-2022-9.

[5] Harter, J. (2022, September 6). *Is quiet quitting real?* Gallup. https://www.gallup.com/workplace/398306/quiet-quitting-real.aspx.

Similarly, another one of the MBA students noted a very common trend that emerges when diversity goals are limited only to recruiting numbers. She described a strong emphasis on including candidates from underrepresented groups in the hiring pipeline for entry-level positions. Unfortunately, little progress was made in terms of improving the diversity of mid- and senior-level management. She indicated that "Diversity needs to be embraced at all levels of the company in order to have a significant positive impact on the organization."

The attraction–selection–attrition model, which states that the people make the place, reveals that attrition is one of the key components of how an organizational culture is perpetuated. So who does an organization keep, and who does it lose? Does it lose certain groups of individuals? And what can we do to minimize the attrition of people from marginalized backgrounds who we really want to retain in our organizations? In this chapter, we present a variety of practices that might help enhance diversity, equity, and inclusion (DEI) by increasing the retention of people from marginalized backgrounds.

Mentoring

Many organizations use mentoring to help employees adapt to, excel in, and advance within the organization. Although mentors can help their mentees in a wide variety of ways, the literature has tended to reduce these ways into two different sets of functions: career-related and psychosocial functions.[6] The career-related or instrumental assistance that mentors provide includes providing opportunities, giving resources, allowing access to networks, protecting, providing developmental experiences, and giving assignment-related advice. The psychosocial-related assistance that mentors provide includes listening, counseling, accepting, role modeling, enhancing

---

[6] Kram, K. E. (1983). Phases of the mentor relationship. *Academy of Management Journal*, 26(4), 608–625.

self-esteem, and friendship. Thus, those engaging in psychosocial mentoring may serve as guides, talking employees through issues and reassuring them that the issues will be resolved.

There are at least two different types of mentoring programs that organizations rely on: formal and informal programs. The typical formal mentoring occurs when an organization specifically develops a program and assigns senior employees as mentors to more junior employees. These relationships are typically guided by organizational objectives so they may be somewhat structured in deadlines and content. Informal mentoring is more relaxed and less structured. Junior employees may not be formally paired—they may seek out individuals because they feel a chemistry or kinship.

Mentoring of many forms can be extremely effective; gaining instrumental and psychosocial support can breed confidence and growth. Valerio and Sawyer examined the common activities in effective mentoring relationships between male mentors and female mentees.[7] Their research found that effective mentors use their authority to push workplace culture toward workplace equality. These mentors think of inclusiveness as part of effective talent management, and they understand that bias is a part of everyday life for many people. These mentors also practice "other-focused leadership" rather than "self-focused leadership." This means that effective mentors center others above themselves in their work processes. Having access to this kind of a mentor helps increase commitment to an organization.

It is important to note that there can be disadvantages to mentoring. One MBA student agreed that mentorship programs are a great way to promote people but a common trap is when "mentors only mentor mentees who are like them, thus stifling diversity." For this reason, it may be fairer and more equitable to create a formal mentoring program in which all are encouraged to participate and someone outside of the relationship does the matching.

---

[7] Valerio, A. M., & Sawyer, K. (2016). A lack of sponsorship is keeping women from advancing into leadership. *Harvard Business Review*.

Sponsoring

The concept of sponsoring is similar to mentoring. One of the main differences between the two is that mentors advise you, whereas sponsors advocate for you. Mentors serve as guides telling you, "You can do it, you can do it," whereas sponsors promote you publicly and tell *others* that you can do it. Sponsors, unlike mentors, often use their blue chips, or social capital, to make connections for you. They are interested in tracking your progress. It's not just a one-time deal or a 1-month sort of relationship. They tend to follow you from career development all the way through to promotion.

This relatively new (or deeper, more involved) type of mentorship seems to be very effective in helping retain and promote diverse employees. As one MBA student described, "My boss was a huge sponsor for me. He fought for my promotions and pay raises. He shared his resources readily and genuinely wanted me to succeed. He was very much a sponsor." Another student stated, "My previous manager was more than an ally. He was a mentor and an advocate—a real sponsor. He gave me the confidence to thrive and the 'wings' to challenge and demand change." These experiences reflect the reality that sponsorship is indeed a key element of advancement in organizations.

Importantly, Herminia Ibarra[8] stressed that women are lacking this deeper form of mentorship and that the lack of sponsorship may keep them from ascending into the highest echelons of leadership. Most chief executive officers (CEOs), Ibarra argued, come from line positions. This is important because men tend to hold more line positions, whereas women tend to switch from line to staff positions as they advance. Thus, more men have experience with profit and loss. In addition, most men get jobs with a larger span of control—they have more direct reports and larger budgets. Finally, men report getting more C-suite visibility than do women. Together, these characteristics mean that there is an uneven playing field

---

[8] Ibarra, H. (2019, August 19). A lack of sponsorship is keeping women from advancing into leadership. *Harvard Business Review*.

where women need more than mentoring—they need *sponsoring*. The same is undoubtedly true for people from other marginalized backgrounds. Although sponsorship can rarely be mandated, it can be thought of as a spectrum. At the most helpful end, sponsors are providing high-visibility opportunities and publicly advocating for women and people of color when they are not in a position to advocate for themselves.

Rania Anderson and David Smith directly explored the question of what men can do to be better mentors and sponsors for women.[9] They noted that one of the unintended implications of the increasing attention to gender harassment that resulted from the #MeToo movement is men's confusion and fear. Senior male executives—all the way up to the Vice President of the United States[10]—reported that they were avoiding one-on-one meetings with women as a risk management strategy. Women went from having limited access to executives to having no access at all. Indeed, sponsors are not benevolent benefactors. They are influential leaders who intentionally invest in, and rely on, the skills and contributions of those they are sponsoring to achieve their own goals and their protégé's highest potential.

Sponsorship can be nurtured through eight basic steps. Sponsors can do the following:

1. Identify high-potential diverse talent.
2. Determine the best opportunities, or what Anderson and Smith call "stretch roles," to develop protégés. These stretch roles involve situations in which protégés will maximally learn, such as deals that involve profit and loss, strategic importance to the business, strategic clients, starting something new, high risk, or solving a business problem.

---

[9] Anderson, R., & Smith, D. G. (2019, August 7). What men can do to be better mentors and sponsors to women. *Harvard Business Review*.

[10] Grossman, J. L. (2017, December 4). *Vice President Pence's "never dine alone with a woman" rule isn't honorable. It's probably illegal*. Vox. https://www.vox.com/the-big-idea/2017/3/31/15132730/pence-women-alone-rule-graham-discrimination.

3. Position the role by providing their protégés with an understanding of the context, expectations, and provision of support so that they are operating under the maximal conditions for success.
4. Provide opportunities for development and support. Hence, they are not just providing the instrumental support but also the psychosocial support.
5. Pave the way for their protégés by introducing them to powerful people.
6. Ensure their protégés receive candid, performance-based feedback. This means that the sponsor balances giving positive feedback with also giving very accurate and honest feedback.
7. Help their protégés persist. They continuously engage with their protégés through all sorts of organizational challenges and setbacks.
8. Champion their protégés' promotions and recognition. Thus, the sponsor–protégé interaction is not meeting once or twice, nor is it a 1-year relationship; rather, it tends to be one that forms early on in the protégé's career and lasts throughout it.

One MBA student described her former boss, a vice president of the company, as a very powerful, experienced man who constantly praised her work and supported her in public. Because he did this publicly, she noticed that other senior colleagues also started to perceive her positively. He was a mentor—not only in offering advice and telling her that the door was open if she ever had any trouble but also in "just making my life at work stratospherically easier." This kind of sponsorship can substantially improve the experiences of people from a variety of marginalized groups.

Creating Employee Resource Groups

Employee resource groups (ERGs) are voluntary, employee-led groups in which organizational members can join together for empowerment or shared experience. These groups are a valuable

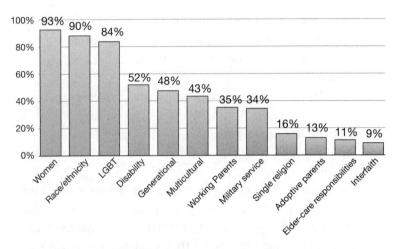

Figure 15.1 Focus areas of ERGs in surveyed companies.
Source: CTR Factor, as cited by Bold Business.

way to help employees, particularly employees from marginalized backgrounds, feel included and have a safe and authentic space. ERGs are often networks that exchange valuable information and knowledge. They can signal that the employer's commitment to diversity is real, that it values employees, and that it provides community and social support for those who are from marginalized backgrounds. Figure 15.1 provides the breakdown of some of the most common ERGs for *Fortune* 500 companies.[11,12]

The influence of ERGs goes way beyond happy hours and special events. ERGs can also push for change within organizations. They can help cultivate mentoring, reduce the biases in certain policies, and put newer employees in touch with senior leaders. That means that ERGs can connect lower level employees to decision-makers in the C-suite and give voices to employees who have ideas that may not otherwise be heard. It is important to understand that ERGs are

---

[11] Bold Business. (2018, September 18). *Gauging the effectiveness of your employee resource group (ERG)*. https://www.boldbusiness.com/society/gauging-effectiveness-your-employee-resource-group.

[12] https://www.ctrfactor.com.

not the only solution that organizations have to managing diversity, and they need to engage the ERG communities with the leaders.

The MBA students in our class had many positive things to say about ERG groups. When asked to describe some workplace initiative that they believed had been successful for them, at least 15 of them mentioned ERGs. The comments included generally positive reactions to ERG, such as "employee resource groups are a great way to create a safe space for minority groups within organizations" and "ERGs are a fantastic resource. I love that they encourage all of their employees to attend, even if they are not part of the specific identity groups." Although some people are concerned that ERGs may work against goals of inclusion by creating divisions or separations between people, it seems that the benefits outweigh the risks.

What do ERGs do that is so successful? Our MBA students indicated a few specific ways in which ERGs can be useful, such as "I think these facilitate plenty of conversation and, because they are not mandatory, remove any perceived 'bureaucratic pressure'" and "Development initiatives within affinity groups (e.g. financial literacy, public speaking) are very effective workplace initiatives." A more in-depth blog[13] highlighted five employers from DiversityInc's 2019 list for ERGs to show what they do:

1. Ernst & Young (E&Y) uses ERGs to help enhance diversity, which E&Y sees as critical to its strategy of innovation and business. E&Y's ERG groups help their employees learn about diversity issues, promote inclusive leadership, provide opportunities for professional development, promote social collaboration and networking, and allow the space for existing members to engage with potential clients.
2. AT&T uses ERGs to engage 130,000 members. The 12 ERGs that the company has are presided over by sponsors who engage in a joint diversity council and act as liaisons who share

---

[13] Pujo, P. (2019, June 13). *Successful employee resource groups: 5 strategies from top companies*. Affirmity. https://www.affirmity.com/blog/employee-resource-groups-5-strategies.

ideas and broadcast attention to important DEI-related issues. Although this may seem similar to most ERGs at other organizations, it is the top-down diversity framework that is built on accountability that makes this ERG so effective.

3. Eli Lilly and Company publishes a book of business conduct[14] that includes ERGs. At Eli Lilly, ERGs educate employees about DEI, create opportunities for diverse employees to feel supported, provide mentoring and networking opportunities, and offer advocacy events and celebrations.
4. Hilton labels ERGs team member resource groups (TMRGs). These TMRGs engage 7,400 employees and focus on growth and development of employee talent, coaching, partnerships with nonprofit organizations as well as minority-owned businesses, and inclusiveness.
5. Northrop Grumman uses ERGs to focus on providing every employee with opportunities to learn more about diversity, better recognize and celebrate diversity, build inclusive leadership skills, and help build community partnerships.

Although these ERGs may be different in their approaches, the commonalities are safe inclusiveness, education for any and all who are interested, and a desire to harness diversity in ways that grow both the individual and the organization.

Enhancing "Safety," Visibility, and Celebrations

Stanford psychologist Claude Steele published a paper referring to an experience that many people from marginalized groups have when they feel "a threat in the air."[15] They look around and see signs

---

[14] Eli Lilly. (2019). *The red book: Code of business conduct.* https://assets.ctfassets.net/srys4 ukjcerm/1L7GvgYYANFe6iA5vmFDmC/a38fba6049822ac75c780ceb1c7fff3b/The-red-book-code-of-business-conduct.pdf.

[15] Steele, C. M. (1997). A threat in the air: How stereotypes shape intellectual identity and performance. *American Psychologist, 52*(6), 613–629. https://doi.org/10.1037/0003-066X.52.6.613.

Figure 15.2 Examples of diversity-welcoming imagery.

that they may not be welcome. So when organizations enhance the psychological safety of their environments, the visibility of diversity within them, and the celebration of perspectives and people who are from minoritized backgrounds, then organizations are essentially reducing these threats in the air by making organizations safe.

There are some very easy ways in which organizations can enhance safety. They can do this by signifying with a very clear object, sticker, or other sign that diversity is welcome. Examples are shown in Figure 15.2.

Organizations can create safe spaces by listing the programs they have very visibly. Similarly, they can list the diversity-related accolades that they have received. For instance, Apple wrote,[16] "Apple has been at the top of [the Human Rights Campaign's Best Places to Work] list since 2002 when only 5% of Corporate Equality Index companies had non-discrimination policies in place for gender identity and zero percent had transgender-inclusive health

---

[16] Gil, L. (2020). *How Apple supports LGBTQ+ during Pride Month and all year long*. iMore. https://www.imore.com/how-apple-supports-lgbtq-during-pride-month-and-all-year-long.

Figure 15.3 Examples of diversity-forward accolades.

care benefits." This can be and is often shown on organizational websites with the Human Rights Campaign (or other designations), as shown in Figure 15.3. All of these accolades and more are ones that Northrop Grumman received in 2021, and the company advertises this on its web page.[17] Organizations can do other things to enhance safety and visibility. They can create all-gender restrooms. They can nurture their employees. And they can foster diversity and use visible signs to reduce "threats in the air." They can print company shirts, celebrate Pride month visibly, and engage in parades (Figure 15.4). Several organizations have done this: IKEA offered limited-edition Pride products as part of its #ProgressIsMade campaign, which advocates for LGBTQ+ inclusion.[18]

---

[17] Northrop Grumman. (2021). *Awards for diversity and inclusion*. https://www.northropgrumman.com/corporate-responsibility/awards-for-diversity-inclusion.

[18] IKEA. (2021). *IKEA U.S. launches Pride campaign to push for greater progress toward LGBTQ+ inclusion*. https://www.ikea.com/us/en/newsroom/corporate-news/ikea-u-s-launches-pride-campaign-to-push-for-greater-progress-toward-lgbtq-inclusion-pubcf8b9e77.

Figure 15.4 Examples of LGBTQ+ positive campaigns.

In addition, organizations can include celebrations of all major holidays. They can make sure they are working with a cultural calendar. They can include diverse decor and ensure that they have educational programs around different cultures. They can have traditional food potlucks or make sure that their parties are nondenominational or inclusive of holidays and events such as Diwali, Ramadan, Hanukkah, Christmas, and the Lunar New Year. They are not taking away people's joy but, rather, they are adding to it. This helps make organizations safe and unthreatening places for everyone.

Diversity Training

Diversity training is often defined as a program or set of programs that attempt to help individuals understand their personal biases, promote dialogue between group members, and provide education about oneself and others in an attempt to get people to work more effectively and safely together. According to McKinsey & Company,[19] U.S. companies spend $8 billion a year on diversity training. There is little doubt that diversity training evokes very strong negative reactions from some individuals. There have been nightmare

---

[19] McKinsey & Company. (2017, April 7). *Focusing on what works for workplace diversity.* https://www.mckinsey.com/featured-insights/gender-equality/focusing-on-what-works-for-workplace-diversity.

stories about bigoted individuals leading training. Some attendees have stated that the content of diversity training was so poor that they emerged more confused than they were before training. Some employees feel very defensive about being forced to attend and told how to think. And many organizations do not seem invested in actually changing anything but, rather, just need to check a box that says they implemented a diversity training program. These and other issues make it clear to us why there are many negative myths surrounding diversity training, which we have written about, and how much work there remains to be done in this area.

You might be surprised to know, then, that we not only think diversity training is important but also think it *should be mandatory* for all employees, from entry level up to CEO. Given the billions that are spent on training each year, one might anticipate that most companies require it. However, the Society of Human Resource Management (SHRM) reports that only 32% of companies actually require some form of DEI training for employees.[20] This percentage is remarkably low given the large number of complaints that seem to exist and the cultural wars that are brewing about being forced to do training.[21] Furthermore, there is mixed evidence in many studies about the benefits of training; a study by Chang and colleagues revealed some favorable outcomes of a short online training program but that White male trainees seem to be impervious to the benefits.[22] Not surprisingly, many negative reactions to mandatory diversity training are from White people; but as *Forbes* author Janice Gassam Asare writes, "If we continue to prioritize those in power, workplace

---

[20] Gurchiek, K. (2021, February 23). *Report: Most companies are "going through the motions" of DEI.* SHRM. https://www.shrm.org/resourcesandtools/hr-topics/behavioral-competencies/global-and-cultural-effectiveness/pages/report-most-companies-are-going-through-the-motions-of-dei.aspx.

[21] Young, C. (2022, September 8). The battle over diversity training. *The Bulwark.* https://www.thebulwark.com/the-battle-over-diversity-training.

[22] Chang, E. H., Milkman, K. L., Grommet, D. M., Rebele, R., Massey, C., Duckworth, A. L., & Grant, A. (2019, July 9). Does diversity training work the way it's supposed to? *Harvard Business Review.* https://hbr.org/2019/07/does-diversity-training-work-the-way-its-supposed-to.

equity will continue to evade us."[23] Indeed, it seems that our research in this area needs to evolve.

To be sure, we have no illusions that diversity training is the silver bullet. How could an hour or two of unlearning bad habits be enough to correct a lifetime of learning bad habits? It is easy to criticize diversity training, and we have done this ourselves. What should we expect of a brief single training episode, typically lasting 1 hour, and often delivered online? Probably not very much, and yet we also know that training more generally (which is essentially education with action) can be very effective. And to that end, a meta-analysis of more than 40 years of research on diversity training has shown that it can be effective, particularly when it targets awareness and skill development, and the training occurs over time.[24] Moreover, our own research has provided evidence for the efficacy of two diversity training exercises—perspective taking, or trying to mentally walk in someone else's shoes (e.g., an LGBT co-worker), and goal setting.[25] For the first longitudinal study, we had individuals in our study write about the perspective of their LGBT or racial minority colleagues and imagine what it must be like for them to experience their day. This action led our trainees to show improved pro-diversity attitudes and behavioral intentions toward these colleagues 8 months post-training. In another study, we also found evidence that goal-setting strategies were effective: When diversity trainees set goals to improve their interactions with particular outgroup members (e.g., "I won't laugh at jokes about X" and "I will attend a supportive meeting for Group X"), research showed that their pro-diversity behaviors improved 3 months after training and their pro-diversity attitudes improved 9 months post-training. We have

---

[23] Gassam Asare, J. (2022, October 7). Have we been wrongfully vilifying DEI training? *Forbes*. https://www.forbes.com/sites/janicegassam/2022/10/07/have-we-been-wrongfully-vilifying-dei-training/?sh=46bfe8183b35.

[24] Bezrukova, K., Spell, C. S., Perry, J. L., & Jehn, K. A. (2016). A meta-analytical integration of over 40 years of research on diversity training evaluation. *Psychological Bulletin, 142*(11), 1227–1274.

[25] Lindsey, A., King, E., Membere, A., & Cheung, H. (2017, July 28). Two types of diversity training that really work. *Harvard Business Review*. https://hbr.org/2017/07/two-types-of-diversity-training-that-really-work.

Table 15.1 Diversity Training Myths

Myth	Reality
Diversity training doesn't work.	It can be effective in achieving some outcomes when designed and implemented appropriately.
Diversity training always leads to backlash.	Meta-analytic work suggests that overall effects are small but neutral to positive.
Diversity is just common sense.	Biases get in the way of objectivity.
Diversity training is about placing the blame on White men.	Good training should benefit everyone.
Anyone can lead diversity training.	Trainers matter—they need specific skills, expertise, and background to be most effective.
Diversity training will be sufficient to create inclusive organizations.	Training should be one of many integrated, strategic efforts to support DEI.
People from marginalized backgrounds should not go to diversity training.	Biases exist within and between many groups; training can be beneficial to everyone.
Diversity training is just like all other kinds of training.	Diversity is a unique topic with specific attitudes and behaviors—much different from typical training programs.

also previously published work[26] that both highlights and provides a summary of evidence describing the errors with some of the most commonly held training-related myths. We provide some of these myths, together with the realities, in Table 15.1.

Nonetheless, we think that diversity training is incredibly important for organizations, and we can best articulate this critical necessity by comparing it to safety training. For employees in a great number of workplace situations—for instance, those working with heavy saws, oil rigs, poisonous chemicals, airplanes, raw chicken,

---

[26] Cheng, S., Corrington, A., Dinh, J., Hebl, M. R., King, E. B., Ng, L., Reyes, D., Salas, E., & Traylor, A. (2018). Challenging diversity training myths: Changing the conversation about diversity training to shape science and practice. *Organizational Dynamics*, 48(4), 100678. https://www.sciencedirect.com/science/article/pii/S0090261618301505.

or thousands of other professions—safety training is not only mandatory by the organization but also required and even enforced by government entities (e.g., the Occupational Safety and Health Administration). This safety training ensures the safety, health, and well-being of employees. By extension, diversity training also ensures conversations about the health and well-being of employees (particularly of those who belong to groups protected by law) and is part of preventing employees from acting in discriminatory ways toward other employees. Training ostensibly teaches us to be aware, how to respect and act toward others, and how we can benefit from differences. Because we are still in our infancy about how best to conduct diversity training, we should not abandon or make it optional (both of which far too many companies have done). Rather, we should consider investing the $8 billion that is spent in this industry to better learn, invest, and produce the most effective training and programming of which we are capable.

Given the very strong backlash that often emerges when companies learn they must institute training or when employees learn they must attend it, diversity training must be strongly empirically based. Here is what we do know about the best science and practice available:

Training as part of DEI strategy: Diversity training is unlikely to have an impact on the day-to-day experiences of people from marginalized backgrounds unless it is part of an integrated DEI strategy with top management support. If organizations want to get serious about ensuring that training influences behavior, they have to ensure the presence, support, and participation of top management buy-in. It's just critical to have ongoing messaging from leadership and to see their visible participation and diversity efforts. This should permeate every decision and action. Management buy-in is not the end goal. It's the starting point.

Tailored diversity training content: We warn readers that a one-size-fits-all diversity training program rarely has lasting impacts. What works in training with one organization doesn't necessarily work with another organization. One organization might have a problem with total lack of diversity at the highest level. Another problem may be a hostile environment. An organization that has no racial diversity but has women equally dispersed in all job positions except for the very top will likely need different elements accentuated in training than an organization with a great deal of racial diversity but whose non-White and women employees are low ranking and incredibly unhappy at work. Thus, we believe that diversity training should be organizationally based and specifically tailored to meet the needs and goals of each company.

Think carefully about training objectives: Educators and scholars of learning have long understood that different instructional strategies should be used depending on learning goals. Is it reasonable to try to change the attitudes, beliefs, and behaviors that people have developed over a lifetime in a single, 1-hour lecture? Probably not.

Evidence from meta-analyses, which are studies that combine the results of many different kinds of studies, suggests that typical diversity training programs can have a positive impact on immediate knowledge but have little effect on behavior over time.[27,28] This means that people generally know more about diversity after they attend the typical 1-hour training session, but they don't necessarily translate that knowledge into behavior. That's probably because these programs are actually (purposefully or not-so-purposefully) designed to increase knowledge. We often tell people about what the laws are regarding harassment, who to talk to at the organization if they believe that they have been targeted by harassment, or sometimes about what unconscious bias is and how it operates. Why

---

[27] Bezrukova, K., Spell, C. S., Perry, J. L., & Jehn, K. A. (2016). A meta-analytical integration of over 40 years of research on diversity training evaluation. *Psychological Bulletin*, 142(11), 1227–1274.

[28] Kalinoski, Z. T., Steele-Johnson, D., Peyton, E. J., Leas, K. A., Steinke, J., & Bowling, N. A. (2013). A meta-analytic evaluation of diversity training outcomes. *Journal of Organizational Behavior*, 34(8), 1076–1104.

would we expect that this kind of training—where we are teaching people about laws and terms—would change behavior?

Consistent with this, a large-scale study on diversity training[29] developed a 1-hour online training course (one on gender bias, another on many different biases, and another control) and administered it to more than 3,000 individuals within a global organization. The content of the training focused on educating others about bias, reflecting on one's own bias, and then learning about ways to overcome bias (e.g., more objectively evaluating resumes and trying to be bias-free on performance evaluations). The researchers found that attitudes toward women improved, particularly for those who started with somewhat negative attitudes toward women prior to training.

However, the behavioral change measure (whether they would later nominate more women for a position) was only effective for women who took the training, not the men. But the effectiveness of being more favorable toward women also spilled over toward having more favorable attitudes toward people from other marginalized groups. When you consider that this training was not particularly focused on the specific organization or the specific problems that the organization might have been suffering from, and that it was not explicitly behaviorally focused, we think it is noteworthy that a 1-hour training session can produce results that are seen 3 weeks later. Although this might be disappointing to some, we are optimistic that we can create more effective, long-lasting, and holistic diversity training. Indeed, research from our lab has determined that integrating goal setting and perspective taking in diversity training sessions can improve relevant outcomes. This means that specifying achievable outcomes and taking time to consider the perspectives of others may be helpful elements of training.

Of course, "one and done" will not create long-term behavioral change. It's important to end this section with a reminder that

---

[29] Chang, E. H., Milkman, K. L., Gromet, D. M., Rebele, R. W., Massey, C., Duckworth, A. L., & Grant, A. M. (2019). The mixed effects of online diversity training. *Proceedings of the National Academy of Sciences of the USA*, *116*(16), 7778–7783.

behavior change of any form takes time, practice, and reinforcement. We need to learn what we should do, practice it, and get feedback about it. The ultimate goal of creating supportive and inclusive organizational cultures is quite distant from the 1-hour discussion of DEI; the dialogue and insistence on positive changes must continue over time.

Self-Assessing and Correcting

An important strategy for ensuring that efforts persist over time is building in systems of continuous assessment and correction. Organizations can collect data on diversity-related efforts, they can try to be transparent about what they learn, and they can identify new goals and objectives. Each of these steps is critical to strategic DEI.

How do organizations best engage in self-assessment? They can do this in a number of ways, beginning with questioning the status quo rather than assuming that the policies and processes that they enacted have had the intended effects. One of the issues that organizations should look for when examining their employees is the structural integration of diversity. Some people call this a DEI audit. This means they can look at the percentage of workers who are from racial/ethnic minority backgrounds, for example, and they want to ensure that these workers are not all stuck at the bottom, as they are in Table 15.2. Ideally, they should be dispersed throughout the organization. That is, they should look more like Table 15.3, in which the percentages are similar, whether the workers are entry-level workers, staff, supervisors, or in middle management or top management positions.

Self-assessment should also include feedback from diverse employees. This could take the form of surveys, focus groups, anonymous hotlines, or interviews—the method matters less than the act of working to identify ongoing needs and opportunities for change. DEI is and should be an ongoing process in which self-assessment and correction are embedded in the fabric of organizational life.

Table 15.2 Inequitable Example of Diversity Spread Within an Organization

	Operations (%)	Marketing and Sales (%)	Accounts and Finance (%)	Human Resources (%)
Top management	0	0	2	3
Middle management	0	3	0	4
Supervisors	5	10	10	13
Entry-level workers/support	50	67	68	60

Table 15.3 Equitable Example of Diversity Spread Within an Organization

	Operations (%)	Marketing and Sales (%)	Accounts and Finance (%)	Human Resources (%)
Top management	30	32	31	32
Middle management	30	25	23	32
Supervisors	30	31	33	25
Entry-level workers/support	33	25	32	31

Integrating all of these programs and practices, together with clear strategy and top management support, may help ensure experiences of inclusion and the retention of people from diverse backgrounds in organizations.

Tools for Working Together

Reflect on your current (or most recent) workplace and consider the following questions:

1. Why do people typically leave your organization?
2. Do certain demographic groups turn over more than others?
3. Which strategies do you think your organization might adopt to reduce attrition?

4. Why do you think the organization has not already adopted these strategies?

We recommend reading the following article published on The Conversation website: https://theconversation.com/the-mental-health-pros-and-cons-of-minority-spaces-in-the-workplace-107554. Afterward, indicate what you have learned about the pros and cons of the movement to try to create safe spaces and safety groups for individuals of all backgrounds.

16
Final Reflections on Working Together

An older person is walking along the beach when she encounters a youngster picking up something and throwing it back into the ocean. The older person asks the youngster what he is doing, to which the youngster responds that he is picking up starfish and throwing them back into the ocean. The tide is going out and if he doesn't throw them back, they will die. The old person looks at the miles and miles of beach and says that there is so much beach and so many starfish that the youngster can't possibly make a difference. The youngster throws a starfish back into the ocean, looks at the old person, and says, "I made a difference for that one." This is one rendition of Eiseley's "The Star Thrower" that has been modified throughout the years.[1] Can you and your actions alone make a difference? YES.

We believe that your actions can make a difference. This difference will depend on your span of control. Some of you may have relatively small spans of control. Perhaps you can influence some of your family members, some good friends, and one or two people in your workplace. But this *is* influence, and we hope that you will take the things that you have learned from this book and use this knowledge to help others work together more inclusively. For others, you may have a more significant span of influence. You may be more influential and/or have larger sets of personal and professional connections within your reach. Or you may even find yourself at the top and have a very significant span of control. Whatever that span is, we want you to be your own star throwers of inclusion. Lex Frieden definitely is.

---

[1] Eiseley, L. (1969). The star thrower. In The *unexpected universe*. Harcourt.

A Star Thrower of Inclusion

Growing up in a farm community where there were hailstorms before harvests and an entire crop could be wiped out in a single day, Lex was used to bad things happening and needing to move on.[2] This would prove useful to Lex, who started out his life in Alva, Oklahoma. He was the typical all-American youth—he played on a state championship golf team in high school, was a lifeguard at the local pool, became an Eagle Scout, and was valedictorian of his high school class. He headed to Oklahoma State University with exciting dreams of becoming an electrical engineer.

Life can change quickly, as it did for Lex 1 week before Thanksgiving break his freshmen year. He was out partying with friends and upon heading back to their dorms, his friend pulled out to pass a vehicle and accidentally hit another one head-on. Everyone in the car had minor injuries. Everyone except for Lex, who put his feet up to brace himself for the impact and broke his neck. When he asked about his future, his doctor suggested he focus on what was above his shoulders. Yes, in an instant, Lex had become a quadriplegic.

Lex took his fortitude and applied to Oral Roberts University, which rejected him, telling him that its policy did not include making accommodations for disabled students on campus.[3] He felt outrage not only over that but also over the outright experiences of discrimination he would experience as the status quo for decades. Business could freely discriminate. Restaurants didn't have to have ramps. Those using wheelchairs had to roll into the street because sidewalks didn't exist or didn't have curb cuts.

---

[2] Burkes, P. (2015, July 26). Executive Q&A: Alva native says research, timing, led him to design nation's historic disability policy. *The Oklahoman*. https://www.oklahoman.com/article/5436124/executive-qa-alva-native-says-research-timing-led-him-to-design-nations-historic-disability-policy.

[3] Tomlinson, C. (2020, February 19). A university denied Lex Frieden admission because he was disabled. Then he fought back. *Houston Chronicle*. https://www.houstonchronicle.com/business/columnists/tomlinson/article/Thirty-years-later-ADA-not-a-handicap-on-business-15065967.php.

There was an accessible building under construction and the deans were happy to accommodate Lex at the University of Tulsa. This undergraduate psychology major graduated and began to study independent living of those with disabilities. Clearly, this young man was destined to change the world. Lex would become one of the main architects of none other than the Americans with Disabilities Act (ADA) of 1990.

Codified by President George H. W. Bush, the ADA represents "one of America's most comprehensive pieces of civil rights legislation."[4] This law

> prohibits discrimination and guarantees that people with disabilities have the same opportunities as everyone else to participate in the mainstream of American life—to enjoy employment opportunities, to purchase goods and services, and to participate in State and local government programs and services.

Thirty years after it was instituted, National Public Radio interviewed a small set of people who are among the millions supported by this law. One stated,

> This law not only can help disabled individuals learn about our rights, but I think also can really foster a sense of dignity and pride within disabled individuals to recognize that we are not the problem, we are not the ones that need to change. It is the society around us.[5]

Dr. Lex Frieden became and is still today a renowned professor and researcher at The University of Texas Health Sciences Center at Houston. More than 30 years after its passage, Lex still marvels at the power that this law had in shifting attitudes, increasing opportunities, and changing lives for those who have a disability.

---

[4] U.S. Department of Justice. (n.d.). *Introduction to the Americans with Disabilities Act.* https://www.ada.gov/ada_intro.htm.
[5] Shapiro, J., & Bowman, J. (2020, July 6). *One laid groundwork for the ADA; The other grew up under its promises.* NPR. https://www.npr.org/2020/07/26/895480926/the-americans-with-disabilities-act-was-signed-into-law-30-years-ago.

Despite a hailstorm, this small-town Oklahoma farm boy rewrote the course of millions of people's lives by examining, writing, promoting, and working to pass protective legislation. We devoted the pages of this book to the ways that individuals and organizations can address bias and create equity. But we must also use this moment to reflect a critical truth: It is legislation—the actions of government bodies—that has great power to address inequity.

Takeaways

In 2020, the Society for Human Resource Management[6] launched a Blue Ribbon Commission on Racial Equity. The report generated by the diverse members of the commission (including Eden) included a common vision that "bias, discrimination and inequity in the workplace are organizational culture issues, and individuals with influence in the workplace must interrupt the systemic process that perpetuates these issues." The commission further asserted that "diversity, equity and inclusion should be part of the overall business strategy and owned by the entire senior leadership team."

It is these messages, grounded in best practice and robust evidence, that we hope you will take away from this book. You now know the realistic, financial, and moral imperatives for diversity, equity, and inclusion (DEI), as well as the individual and organizational underpinnings of bias. You can identify individual and organizational strategies for addressing bias as well as methods for enhancing DEI across the talent management cycle. Anti-bias policies and practices, if enforced and supported by leaders and allies, will help create organizations with less bias. Laws that safeguard the inherent dignity of all will create a society in which human rights are cherished.

But how will you use this knowledge? Buddhist teachings expand the opportunity for change beyond a single starfish by reminding

---

[6] Society for Human Resource Management. (2021). *Blue Ribbon Commission on Racial Equity manifesto.* https://togetherforwardatwork.shrm.org/brc.

us that a thousand candles can be lit from one flame. One person—*you*—can be the flame that ignites change in your organization. We hope you light that flame.

Tools for Working Together

Please spend a little time thinking about what you have learned from reading this book. We would ask you to reflect on five specific goals that you have toward DEI. What behaviors and/or strategies can you specifically commit to adopting to make your workplace more diverse and inclusive? Describe all five of these goals in detail on paper. Remember to make them SMART goals. Consider sharing all five of these goals with others. Your actions can and will make a difference.

Index

For the benefit of digital users, indexed terms that span two pages (e.g., 52–53) may, on occasion, appear on only one of those pages.

Tables, figures, and boxes are indicated by *t, f,* and *b* following the page number

accounting profession, 95–96
accounts and finance
   equitable example of diversity spread within, 195*t*
   inequitable example of diversity spread within, 195*t*
acknowledgement
   identity, 103–4
   stigma, across time of interview, 105*f*
action, allies confronting discrimination, 118–21
Adelson, Edward H., 57–58
   checkerboard illusion, 58
   checker-shadow illusion, 57*f*, 57–58
   checker-shadow illusion, cropped, 57*f*, 57–58
Adelson, Sheldon, 2
Adichie, Chimamanda Ngozi, 68
advertising
   racism in, 86–87
   reducing failures, 31–32
   Van Heusen racist, of 1950s, 88*f*
Age Discrimination and Employment Act, 72
Age Discrimination in Employment Act, 21
Akhtar, Mohammed, 67–68
allies
   acronym for ALLIES, 125*f*, 125
   actions to confront discrimination, 118–21
   assuming and using psychological standing, 121–24
   configuration of participants in Asch's study, 117*f*
   conformity in social psychology experiment, 116–18, 117*f*
   education and awareness, 115–16
   effective behaviors for, 120*b*
   fighting conformity, 116–18
   ineffective behaviors for, 122*b*
   LGBTQ+ co-workers and, 112
   standing up in absence of targets, 124–25
   supporting Black colleagues, 127*b*
   tools for working together, 125–27
American Sign Language, 158–59
Americans with Disabilities Act (ADA), 128
   Bush (G. H. W.) and, 199
   Lex Frieden and, 199
anchoring bias, 56
Anderson, Rania, on mentoring women, 180
Ann B. Hopkins v. Price Waterhouse (1987), 100
Apple, Human Rights Campaign's Best Places to Work list, 185–86
Apple Health, 32–33
ASA. *See* attraction, selection, and attrition (ASA) model
Asian people
   phenomenon of bamboo ceiling, 83
   U.S. population, 23–24
   workers avoiding conflict, 44–45

AT&T, employee resource groups (ERGs), 183–84
Athleta, 11
attitudes, prejudice and, 67–68
attraction, selection, and attrition (ASA) model, 148–49
Auger-Dominguez, Daisy, 8
Authentic Brands Group LLC, 86–87
authenticity, concept of, 14–15
awareness, allies, 115–16

baby boomer death clock, 20
Bader Ginsburg, Ruth
  Nomadic Boys on, 113
  Scalia and, 45–46
bamboo ceiling, phenomenon of, 83
Barbie, 31
Barrica, Andrew, #MeToo movement, 141
Belichick, Bill, 9
belief, 1–2
belonging, importance of, 15
Biased (Eberhardt), 138
biases, 2, 51–53
  anchoring, 56
  comparing co-workers and self, 60–61
  fat suits studying obesity, 55, 78, 107
  identity-hidden reviews and interviews, 164–66
  illusions and, 60
  job descriptions, 156–57
  mental shortcuts, 56–61
  obesity, 55–56
  prejudice, 65–68
  self-serving, 61
  similarity effect, 79
  similar-to-me, 163
  stereotypes, 61–65
  tools for working together, 68–69
  unorthodox applicants for hiring, 166–69
  vehicle stereotypes, 61–65, 62*f*
  See also stereotypes
Bitty and Beau's Coffee, 128–29

Black community, accounting profession, 96
Black Entertainment Television, 31
Black musicians, identity-hidden reviews, 165
Black people, racial reckoning, 97–98
Black Student Association, 115
Bland, Sandra, death of, 145, 146, 147
Blue Ribbon Commission on Racial Equity, 200
Bohnet, Iris, video on gender bias, 174
Bono, Chaz, 112–13
Bostock v. Clayton County, Georgia (2020), 26
Burberry, 32–33
burnout, job frustration, 175–76
Bush, George H. W., Americans with Disabilities Act (ADA) of 1990, 199
business imperative
  DEI, 10
  See also financial imperative of diversity

café wall optical illusion, 59*f*, 59
California, mandating paid family leave, 23
Cambridge Dictionary, diversity definition, 11–12
career advancement, organizational biases, 91–93
Care for All DEI report, Zoom, 4
Carnegie, Andrew, 2
Catalyst, 82
Center for Audit Quality, 96
certified public accountants (CPAs), 95–96
Chapman, Tracy, "Talkin' Bout a Revolution," 96–97
Charlottesville Unite the Right, 137
checkerboard illusion, Adelson's, 58
checker-shadow illusion, Adelson's, 56–58, 57*f*
Cher, Nomadic Boys on, 112–13
Chicago Public School System, pandemic and, 175

chief executive officers (CEOs), 22
Christianity, United States, 24–25
Chugh, Dolly, 118–19
Civil Rights Act, Title VII, 72
Civil Rights Act of 1991, 72
class-action lawsuit, Sterling
	Jewelers, 52
Coca-Cola, 74
Colorado, mandating paid family
	leave, 23
comfort zones, diversity removing
	people from, 46
communications, reducing failures, 33
compensation, organizational
	biases in, 90
conflict
	differing views causing, 45–46
	diversity leading to, 46–47
conformity, allies fighting, 116–18
confrontation, discrimination, 108–9
Connecticut, mandating paid family
	leave, 23
constructive disruption, notion
	of, 129–30
Conversation, The, article on
	website, 196
corporate social responsibility (CSR), 42
	moral imperative of diversity, 39–41
correction, reducing employee
	attrition, 194–95
COVID-19 pandemic, 44–45
	challenges of working mother
		during, 175
	confusion and blame over origin of, 67
	missing child care infrastructure, 158
	organization accommodations, 128
	quiet quitting during, 175–76
	workforce participation, 21–22
Crandall, Chris, 45
Creamalicious, Walmart and, 29
Cyrus, Miley, 114

Daboll, Brian, 9
Danger, Laura, coping during
	pandemic, 175

deep-level characteristics, diversity,
	12–13, 17
DEI. *See* diversity, equity, and
	inclusion (DEI)
DeJoria, John Paul, 2
Delaware, mandating paid family
	leave, 23
demography
	changes in organizations, 18–19
	changes suggesting future in
		purchasing power trends, 31
Designing for the Digital Age
	(Goodwin), 70, 71*f*
Dick's Sporting Goods, Hobart of, 150–51
disclosure, identity, 104–5
discomfort, embracing, for DEI, 7
discrimination
	adverse impact, 72–73
	allies confronting, 118–21
	confronting, 108–9
	employee turnover, 34–35
	financial imperative for
		diversity, 34–35
	lost opportunity, 35
	organizations' target of
		dismantling, 137–38
	overt, 70–74
	prejudice and, 67–68
	reducing justifications for
		others', 106–7
	retaliation, 73
	sexual harassment, 73
	subtle, 74–83
	targets compensating, 107–8
	targets of, debunking stereotypes, 107
	underreporting of, 73–74
	U.S. Equal Employment Opportunity
		Commission (EEOC), 73
	See also allies; individual-level
		discrimination; individual targets
		of discrimination; organization-
		level discrimination; subtle
		discrimination
District of Columbia, mandating paid
	family leave, 23

Index

diversity
  Cambridge Dictionary definition, 11–12
  deep-level characteristics, 12–13, 17
  definition of, 13
  guide for, 2
  level differentiation, 13
  Pisters of MD Anderson, 134–35
  recruiting and, 176–77
  surface-level characteristics, 12–13, 17
  word, 6
  See also downsides of diversity
diversity, equity, and inclusion (DEI), 3
  curiosity on, 6
  embracing discomfort for, 7
  Hobart of Dick's Sporting Goods on, 150–51
  imperatives of, 10, 43
  initiatives in organizations, 141–44
  projecting authentic optics, 153f, 153–54
  sharing book on, 4
  support in Texas, 150, 151
  transforming organizations, 146–48
  women in candidate pool, 151–52
"Diversity and Authenticity," 14–15
"Diversity as Strategy" (Thomas), 129–30
"Diversity Doesn't Stick Without Inclusion" (Sherbin and Rashid), 14
DiversityInc, employee resource groups (ERGs), 183–84
diversity training
  DEI strategy, 191
  evidence from meta-analyses, 192–93
  focusing on objectives, 192
  importance for organizations, 190–91
  large-scale study on, 193
  measuring behavioral change with, 193–96
  myths, 190t
  reducing employee attrition, 187–94
  research on, 189–90
  science and practice available, 191–92
  tailoring content, 191–92
Dobbs, 26
Doerr, John, focusing on metrics, 173
doing the right thing, moral imperative of diversity, 41–42
Dolce & Gabbana, 32–33
Dollywood Splash Country, 113–14
downsides of diversity
  comfort zones, 46
  hard work of DEI, 49
  MBA students on, 49
  mistrust, miscommunication, and conflict, 46–47
  negative reactions, 47–48
  resistance, 47
  tools for working together, 49–50
  unprepared workers, 48–49
Down syndrome, 34, 128–29
Dropbox, paid leave for workers, 157–58
Duguid, Michelle, learning about bias, 100–1

Eberhardt, Jennifer, on Nextdoor, 138
education
  allies, 115–16
  bifurcation in levels in U.S., 26–28
Electrolux, advertising, 31–32
Eli Lilly and Company, employee resource groups (ERGs), 184
Ellevest Investing, 31
Ely, Robin, studying diversity, 36
Emerson Automation Solutions, 3
employee attraction
  explicit communication about diversity recruitment, 154–55
  implicit communication about diversity recruitment, 156–57
  projecting authentic DEI optics, 153–54

recruitment tools and strategies, 152
  strategically located
    recruitment, 152–53
  supportive policies for, 157–59
  tools for working together, 159–60
  websites depicting Black vs. White
    employees, 153*f*
employee attrition reduction
  creating employee resource groups
    (ERGs), 181–84, 182*f*
  diversity-forward accolades, 186*f*
  diversity training, 187–94
  diversity training myths, 190*t*
  diversity-welcoming imagery, 185*f*
  enhancing "safety," visibility, and
    celebrations, 184–87
  equitable example of diversity spread
    within organization, 194, 195*t*
  inequitable example of diversity
    spread within organization,
    194, 195*t*
  LGBTQ+ positive campaigns, 187*f*
  mentoring, 177–78
  self-assessing and correcting, 194–95
  sponsoring, 179–81
  tools for working together, 195–96
employee resource groups (ERGs)
  AT&T, 183–84
  Eli Lilly and Company, 184
  employers from DiversityInc's 2019
    list for, 183–84
  Ernst & Young (E&Y), 183
  focus areas of, 182*f*
  Hilton, 184
  influence of, 182–83
  Northrop Grumman, 184
  reducing employee attrition, 181–84
  success of, 183
  See also employee attrition reduction
employee selection
  behavioral samples, 171–72
  conducting identity-hidden
    reviews, 164–66
  considering unorthodox
    applicants, 166–69

defining job criteria a priori, 162–63
focus on metrics, 173
questions for unstructured and
  structured interviews, 170*b*
re:Work approach, 171
tools for working together, 174
using structured interviews, 169–71
employee turnover,
  discrimination, 34–35
Equal Employment Opportunity
  Commission (EEOC), U.S.,
  73, 128
Equal Pay Act, 72
equity, definition of, 13–14
Ernst & Young (E&Y), employee
  resource groups (ERGs), 183
Etsy, paid leave for workers, 157–58

Facebook, 87, 88–89
fat suits, studying obesity, 55, 78,
  107
Felix, Allyson, 11
financial imperative of diversity, 200
  business organization, 29–34
  complications, 36–37
  discrimination, 29–30, 34–35
  favorable outcomes of, 29–30,
    35–36
  tools for working together, 37–38
fit, job criteria, 163
Flores, Brian, 9, 11
Floyd, George, death of, 145
Fortune 500 companies, 22, 82
  creating employee resource groups
    (ERGs), 181–82
  employee selection, 168–69
  policies attracting workers, 157–58
Frieden, Lex
  Americans with Disabilities Act
    (ADA) of 1990, 199
  Oklahoma State University, 198
  Oral Roberts University, 198
  star thrower of inclusion, 197
  University of Texas Health Sciences
    Center, 199–200

Gallup poll, on quiet quitting, 175–76
Gass, Michelle, Levi's CEO, 62f, 62
Gassam Asare, Janice, on diversity training, 188–89
gender
 identity-hidden reviews, 164
 job descriptions, 156–57
 pay gap in workplace, 22
 video of, bias, 174
 women in the workplace, 21–22
gender identity
 needs analysis, 130
 United States, 26
Glassdoor, "Best Places to Work," 4
goal setting
 organizations, 132–34
 SMART acronym, 133–34
 SWOT analysis, 133–34
Goodwin, Kim, 70, 71f
Google re:Work
 components of approach, 171
 website, 174
Grant, Adam
 culture in hiring, 163
 discrimination, 100–1
Great Depression, 19
Great Resignation, Klotz on, 175–76
Gucci, 32–33

harassment, 52–53
hard work, creating and sustaining DEI, 49
Harvard, 161
Harvard Business Review (journal), 136–37, 146
hepeating, term, 70
heuristics, term, 58
Hewlett Packard, policies attracting workers, 157–58
Hill County Farms, 74
Hilton, employee resource groups (ERGs), 184
Hispanic people, U.S. population, 23–24

Hobart, Lauren, CEO of Dick's Sporting Goods, 150–51
Hopkins, Ann, 99–100
human resources (HR)
 DEI programs, 147–48
 diversity for organization, 135
 equitable example of diversity spread within, 195t
 inequitable example of diversity spread within, 195t
Human Rights Campaign, Apple on 'Best Places to Work' list, 185–86

Ibarra, Herminia, women and sponsorship/mentorship, 179–80
IBM, 130, 137
identities, 12
 acknowledging, 103–4, 104f, 105f
 conducting identity-hidden reviews/interviews, 164–66
 disclosing, 104–5
 individuating, 105–6
 passing or covering, 102–3
IKEA, Pride products, 185–86
immigrant makeup, U.S. population, 23–24
Implicit Associations Test, 6
Incendar, 20
inclusion, definition of, 14
inclusion office, Virginia Commonwealth University, 12
individual-level discrimination, 70
 adverse impact, 72–73
 mansplaining, 70
 on mansplaining, 70, 71f
 overt discrimination, 70–74
 problems of subtle discrimination, 84
 retaliation, 73
 sexual harassment, 73
 subtle discrimination, 74–83
 subtle discrimination in getting the interview, 77–79
 subtle discrimination in performance management and development, 80–81

subtle discrimination in promotion to leadership, 81–83
subtle discrimination in the interview, 79–80
tools for working together, 84–85
underreporting of, 73–74
See also discrimination
individual targets of discrimination, 99–101, 110–11
acknowledging, 103–4, 104*f*, 105*f*
compensating, 107–8
confronting, 108–9
debunking others' stereotypes, 107
disclosing, 104–5
individuating, 105–6
passing or covering, 102–3
reducing justifications for others' discrimination, 106–7
remembering, 109–10
tools for working together, 111
influence
making a difference, 197, 200–1
span of control, 197
ingredient-laden salad, notion of, 16
innovation, team diversity and, 35–36
intersectional identities, 8
interview(s)
conducting identity-hidden reviews and, 164–66
stigma acknowledgement across time, 105*f*
subtle discrimination in, 79–80
subtle discrimination in getting, 77–79
using structured, for employee selection, 169–71
Ivory Tower, academia, 91–92
Ivy League schools
identity-hidden reviews and interviews, 165
recruitment strategies, 89
stereotype in employee selection, 166

Jackson, Michael, "Man in the Mirror," 96–97
JAMA Pediatrics (journal), 33
Jared the Galleria of Jewelry, class-action lawsuit, 52
job
organizational biases in compensation, 90
organizational biases in getting a, 89
organizational biases in promotion, 91–93
Juneteenth National Independence Day, 29

Kahneman, Danny, 58
Kay Jewelers, class-action lawsuit, 52
Keane, Margaret, Synchrony, 62*f*, 62
Kentucky Fried Chicken, advertising, 31–32
Klotz, Anthony, on The Great Resignation, 175–76
Knight, Rebecca, on bias in hiring process, 162–63

labor force, U.S. population and, 19
leadership
diversity, equity, and inclusion (DEI) initiatives, 141–44
subtle discrimination in promotion to, 81–83
level differentiation, diversity, 13
Levi's, Gass as CEO, 62*f*, 62
LGBTQ+ population, 100
diversity-forward accolades, 186*f*
diversity-welcoming imagery, 185*f*
needs analysis, 130
positive campaign examples, 187*f*
United States, 26
See also allies
LinkedIn, 150, 152–53
Lululemon, paid leave for workers, 157–58

McKinsey & Company
diversity training by U.S. companies, 187–88
organizational diversity, 30
"Man in the Mirror," Jackson, 96–97

mansplaining
    schematic of, 71*f*
    term, 70
manterrupting, term, 70
marginalized individuals, 8
marketing and sales
    equitable example of diversity spread within, 195*t*
    inequitable example of diversity spread within, 195*t*
Mary Kay, 31
Maryland, mandating paid family leave, 23
Maslow, Abraham, 2
Massachusetts, mandating paid family leave, 23
Massachusetts Institute of Technology, 57–58
Mayse, Adrian, 95–96
MD Anderson, Pisters of, 134–35
Measure What Matters (Doerr), 173
melting pot
    metaphor, 16, 17
    United States as, 16
mentoring
    formal and informal, 178
    "other-focused" rather than self-focused leadership, 178
    reducing employee attrition, 177–78
    sponsoring and, 179
meritocracy
    illusion of, 2
    myth of, 2
    principle of, 1
    systems of, 2
meritocratic ideal, 2
metaphors
    ingredient-laden salad, 16
    melting pot, 16, 17
    salad bowl, 16, 17
#MeToo movement, 141
    resulting men's confusion and fear, 180
metrics, employee selection, 173

mistrust and miscommunication, diversity leading to, 46–47
Mitsubishi
    hepeating, manterrupting and mansplaining, 70
    hostile setting for women, 51–52
moral imperative of diversity, 200
    corporate social responsibility (CSR), 39–41
    DEI, 10
    on doing the right thing, 41–42
    tools for working together, 42–43
more good, notion of, 40
"motherhood penalty," 15
mothers, in workplace, 23
Munsterberg's illusion, 59*f*, 59
Muslims, United States, 24–25
Myers, Verna, party analogy, 14–15

National Association of Black Accountants (NABA, Inc.), 96
National Association of Colored Women (NACW), 109–10
National Football League (NFL), 9–10, 11
National Public Radio (NPR), 199
needs analysis, organizational, 130–31, 132*b*
need to belong, 15
negative reactions, diversity leading to, 47–48
Netflix, paid leave for workers, 157–58
New Jersey, mandating paid family leave, 23
New York, mandating paid family leave, 23
New York Giants, 9
New York Times, The (newspaper), 22, 110–11
Nextdoor, Eberhardt on, 138
Nigeria, negative outcomes of diversity, 44–45
Nike, 11
Nomadic Boys, 112–13

non-Hispanic White people, U.S. population, 23–24
Northrop Grumman
  accolades for, 185–86
  employee resource groups (ERGs), 184

Obergefell v. Hodges (2015), 113
obesity
  biases, 55–56
  fat suits for studying, 55, 78, 107
Oklahoma State University, 198
operations
  equitable example of diversity spread within, 195*t*
  inequitable example of diversity spread within, 195*t*
Oral Roberts University, 198
Oregon, mandating paid family leave, 23
organization-level discrimination
  organizational biases in compensation, 90
  organizational biases in getting the job, 89
  organizational biases in promotion, 91–93
  tools for working together, 93–94
  See also discrimination
organizations
  celebrations and culture, 187
  DEI efforts for transforming, 146–48
  DEI initiatives for, 141–44
  DEI initiatives transcending, 136
  demographic change in, 18–19
  diversity-forward accolades, 185–86, 186*f*
  diversity training by U.S. companies, 187–88
  diversity-welcoming imagery of, 185*f*, 185
  equitable example of diversity spread within, 195*t*
  goal setting, 132–34
  importance of belonging, 15
  inequitable example of diversity spread within, 195*t*
  messaging of, and backed up by corporate actions, 136–37
  needs analysis, 130–31, 132*b*
  pregnant women, mothers and new parents in, 23
  projecting authentic DEI optics, 153*f*, 153–54
  reflection questions for needs analysis, 132*b*
  self-assessing and correcting, 194–95
  SWOT analysis for goals, 133–34, 139
  SWOT analysis worksheet, 139*f*
  targeting the dismantling of discrimination, 137–38
  tools for working together, 139
  top management buy-in and participation, 134–36
organizational biases, 88–89
  in compensation, 90
  in getting the job, 89
  in promotion, 91–93
  tools for working together, 93–94
organizational diversity
  business advantage, 29–34
  changing demographics suggesting trends, 31
  complications of, 36–37
  new product development and success, 31
  reducing advertising failures, 31–32
  reducing communication failures, 33
  reducing product failures, 32–33
organizational needs analysis, 130–31, 132*b*
Oubre, Greg, elementary school teacher, 62*f*, 62
overt discrimination, individual-level, 70–74

Padilla, Greg, high school teacher, 62*f*, 62
paid family leave, state mandating, 23

parents, new, in workplace, 23
Parents, Family, and Friends of Lesbians and Bays (PFFLG), 112–13
Parton, Dolly, Nomadic Boys on, 113–14
party analogy, Myers', 14–15
Patagonia
  corporate social responsibility (CSR) of, 39–40
  Fair Trade Certified label, 39–40
  Macro Puff Quilt, 39
  PertexR Quantum, 39
Patagonia Worn Wear, 39–40
pay. *See* compensation
pay gap, workplace, 22
people with disabilities
  accommodating, 129
  coffee shop employing, 128–29
  DEI in recruitment, 158–59
Pepsi, advertising, 31–32
performance management and development, subtle discrimination in, 80–81
Person You Mean to Be, The (Chugh), 118–19
Pew Research Center, 18–19, 24–25
Phillips, Kathy, on innovation, 35–36
physical well-being, 15
Pisters, Peter, MD Anderson, 134–35
population growth, declining, in U.S., 19–20
Prada, 32–33
pregnancy belly, subtle discrimination and, 78
Pregnancy Discrimination Act, 72
prejudice, 52–53
  attitudes and discrimination, 67–68
  stereotype content model, 66–67
  stereotypes and, 65–68
  See also biases
Pride month celebrations, 185–86
Procter & Gamble, film on discrimination, 75
product(s)
  development and success of new, 31
  reducing failures, 32–33

#ProgressIsMade campaign, 185–86
promotion, organizational biases in, 91–93
Propublica, 87
psychological standing, allies assuming and using, 121–24
psychological well-being, 15
Pulse nightclub, 112
PVH Corp. (Phillips-Van Heusen Corporation), 86

queen bee phenomenon, stern female leaders, 62–63, 63*t*
quiet quit, 175–76

racial makeup U.S. population, 23–24
racial reckoning, Black people, 97–98
racism, advertising, 86–87
rags-to-riches stories, 2
"Rainbowland," Parton and Cyrus, 114
realistic imperative of diversity, 200
  aging workforce in U.S., 20–21
  bifurcation in education levels, 26–28
  declining population growth, 19–20
  DEI, 10
  demographic change in U.S., 18–19
  disability in workforce, 25
  pregnant women, mothers, and new parents in workplace, 23
  racial and immigrant makeup of U.S. population, 23–24
  religious preferences, 24–25
  sexuality and gender identity, 26
  tools for working together, 28
  women in the workplace, 21–22
recruitment
  diversity, 176–77
  strategically located, 152–53
  tools and strategies, 152
  See also employee attraction
Rehabilitation Act, 72
religious preferences
  employers considering needs of, 159
  U.S. population, 24–25

Rent the Runway, 31
resistance, diversity leading to, 47
Rhode Island, mandating paid family leave, 23
Roe v. Wade, overturn of, 150–51
"Rooney Rule," NFL's, 9
Russia Winter Olympics, 112–13

Saasbee, 5
salad bowl, metaphor, 16, 17
salary.com, 90
Sandberg, Sheryl, discrimination, 100–1
Scalia, Antonin, Ginsburg and, 45–46
Schneider, Ben, organizational culture, 148
Schultz, Howard, 2
self-assessment, reducing employee attrition, 194–95
sexism, subtle discrimination extending, 83
sexuality, United States, 26
sexual orientation, needs analysis, 130
Shoney's, 74
similarity effect, overarching bias, 79
similar-to-me bias, 163
SMART acronym, goal setting, 133–34
Smith, David, on mentoring women, 180
social psychology experiment, study of conformity, 116–18, 117*f*
Society for Human Resource Management (SHRM), 63–64, 188–89, 200
socioeconomic status (SES), differences in, 27–28
span of control, 197
Spanx, 31
sponsoring
  basic steps of, 180–81
  concept of, 179
  reducing employee attrition, 179–81
  stretch roles, 180
Staples, Brent, 110–11
"Star Thrower, The" (Eiseley), 197

Steele, Claude, 110–11, 184–85
Stein, Bob, 172
STEM (science, technology, engineering, and mathematics), stereotypical exemplars, 67
stereotypes, 2, 52–53
  chief executive officers (CEOs), 62, 62*f*
  debunking others', 107
  job descriptions, 156–57
  labels for stern male and female leaders, 63*t*
  older workers, 64–65
  perceptions of competence and warmth, 65, 66*f*
  stereotype content model, 65
  vehicle, 61–65, 62*f*
  See also biases
Sterling Jewelers, class-action lawsuit against, 52
Stitchfix, 31
"Stop Making the Business Case for Diversity" (Georgeac and Rattan), 37
subtle discrimination, 74–83
  in getting the interview, 77–79
  illustrations of experiences, 76–77
  in the interview, 79–80
  in performance management and development, 80–81
  problems of, 84
  in promotion to leadership, 81–83
surface-level characteristics, diversity, 12–13
Synchrony, Keane as CEO, 62*f*, 62

talent management cycle, DEI initiatives, 141, 144
"Talkin' Bout a Revolution," Chapman, 96–97
Taylor, Breonna, death of, 145
team diversity, favorable outcomes of, 35–36
TED talks, 5
TedX talk, Chimamanda Ngozi Adichie, 68

Terrell, Mary Church, National Association of Colored Women (NACW), 109–10
Texas, DEI support, 150, 151
Thomas, Clarence, 26
Thomas, David
"Diversity as Strategy," 129–30
studying diversity, 36
Thomas-Hunt, Melissa, learning about bias, 100–1
Tommasini, Anthony, identity-hidden reviews, 165
tools for working together, 201
actions for individual targets, 111
actions for organizations, 139
allies, 125–27
attraction, selection, and attrition (ASA) model, 148–49
downsides to diversity, 49–50
employee attraction, 159–60
employee selection, 174
financial imperative of diversity, 37–38
identifying diversity, 17
individual-level discrimination, 84–85
moral imperative of diversity, 42–43
organization-level discrimination, 93–94
psychological explanations for bias, 68–69
realistic imperative of diversity, 28
reducing employee attrition, 195–96

United Nations, Watson at, 121
United States
Age Discrimination in Employment Act, 21
aging workforce in, 20–21
bifurcation in education levels, 26–28
Bureau of Labor Statistics, 18–19, 25
Census Bureau, 18–19, 20
declining population growth, 19–20
disability in workforce, 25
diversity training by companies in, 187–88
Equal Employment Opportunity Commission (EEOC), 73, 128
justices Ginsburg and Scalia, 45–46
Marine Corps, 156
melting pot, 16
pregnant women, mothers, and new parents in workplace, 23
racial and immigrant makeup of, 23–24
religious preferences in, 24–25
sexuality and gender identity in, 26
University College of London, Klotz of, 175–76
University of Texas Health Sciences Center, 199–200
unprepared workers, diversity leading to, 48–49

Van Heusen
advertising, 86
modern clothing models, 87f
racist advertisement (1950s), 86, 88f
Vice Media, Auger-Dominguez at, 8
Virginia Commonwealth University, inclusion office at, 12
Vogue Business (magazine), 32–33

Walmart
discrimination, 34
diversity recruitment, 155
Juneteenth National Independence Day, 29
Washington, mandating paid family leave, 23
Watson, Emma, at United Nations, 121
Weinstein, Harvey, 141
Wells Fargo, 9–10
Wharton, 161
When I Grow Up, I Want to Be an … Accountant (Mayse), 95–96
Whistling Vivaldi (Steele), 110–11

Whiting, Sarah, promotion to dean position, 166
Winfrey, Oprah, 2
women
  biases, 51–53
  candidate pool diversity, 151–52
  career advancement, 91–92
  class-action lawsuit against Sterling Jewelers, 52
  compensation of, 90
  cumulative lifetime earnings for men vs., 168f
  experiences of men vs., 168
  "holes" or "gaps" in resumes, 167
  hostile work environment, 51
  lacking mentoring and sponsorship, 179–80
  on men being better mentors and sponsors for, 180
  Mitsubishi has hostile setting, 51–52
  stereotype of "queen bee," 62–63, 63t
  workplace, 21–22
Women's Sports Foundation, 11
workforce, aging, in U.S., 20–21
Working Mother Research Institute, 114
working together, tools for. *See* tools for working together
workplace
  being authentic in, 15
  discrimination, 34
  hostile setting for women, 51
  pregnant women, mothers and new parents in, 23
  sexuality and gender identity in, 26
  women in, 21–22
World Economic Forum, 23
Wright, Amy, coffee shop employing people with disabilities, 128–29

Yuan, Eric, CEO of Zoom, 4, 100–1

Zales, class-action lawsuit, 52
Zoom, Yuan as CEO, 5, 100–1
Zoom Cares, 5
Zoom talks, 5